$\mathcal{A}$
RABBI'S
$\mathcal{J}ourney$
to
HEAVEN

FELIX HALPERN

A RABBI'S *Journey to* HEAVEN

A MIRACULOUS STORY OF
ONE MAN'S *Journey to Heaven*
AND
YOUR 30-DAY *Glory Transformation*

It's Supernatural! Press and Messianic Vision Inc.

Book design by Terry Clifton

ISBN 13 TP: 978-0-7684-6144-2

ISBN 13 eBook: 978-0-7684-6145-9

For Worldwide Distribution, Printed in the U.S.A.

3 4 5 6 7 8 / 25 24 23 22 21

ACKNOWLEDGMENTS

I am eternally grateful to the Lord for restoring my life and returning me to the land of the living. To be able to see into the eyes of my dear wife Bonnie, daughters Heather and Tara, and my grandson Hudson captures the fullness of my heart. They have stood patiently at my side over the course of an entire year as I adjusted back to mortal life, having to adjust to all of my changes.

I am also grateful for a handful of dear confidantes that allowed me to weed through the unknown territory of experiencing death and life. I thank Sid Roth for his daily words of wisdom and availability when I found myself in uncharted waters.

I am also grateful for Carole and Sal Miliziano for their careful editing. I thank my daughter Heather for her editing and her dedication to this work.

CONTENTS

PREFACE

ONE SEPTEMBER MORNING CHANGED EVERYTHING. A quiet moment in time. Like any given moment in a day, week, or month, this one would leave me confronting my final resting place. I would visit Heaven and see things that I have always read about and pondered and dreamt about. I would also see the lower realm, the second heaven, the place where demons dwell. I will share about what I have learned from both.

It all happened suddenly.

In a twinkling of an eye in fact.

My last words and actions to Bonnie were, as always, a kiss and *"I'll see you in the morning."* But the morning never came, at least not the way it normally did. That morning my heart would stop beating, and Heaven would become my resting place.

The changes from my journey to Heaven I now carry with me. I can close my eyes, squeeze them shut tight, as if that will make all of this go away. But when I open them again, it does not.

As a result, I wrote this book with the purpose of sharing keys to living in our Father's glory, following my time in the third heaven after my life-and-death experience in 2019.

I do not presume to believe my experience is a measuring stick for others either. Mine was likely lesser than others, but likely greater than some. Compared to the apostle Paul or John, all of ours are a minimal invasion of Heaven. But everyone's experience is different!

One final note, at the end of this writing you will receive a miracle ingredient for your prayer time: *30 Days in His Glory Meditations and Devotional.* It's a secret that's been hiding right under our noses for years, which miraculously targets one significant area—the soul. Add it into your day first thing in the morning for 30 days, and you will discover this gift.

If you choose to accept this mission, you also will follow in the words of the psalmist in 96:7-8, *"Ascribe to the Lord glory and strength. Ascribe to the Lord the glory due his name."*

INTRODUCTION

THERE HAVE BEEN NUMEROUS BOOKS WRITTEN ABOUT individuals who have experienced the glory of Heaven. All portray a divine masterpiece of perfection. A glory-filled place of extraordinary beauty. To the natural mind it is incomprehensible.

As a Messianic rabbi and Jewish believer in Yeshua, Messiah, a world was discovered that our ancient forefathers longed for and our sages spoke of, a world that awaits all of us as our eternal destination.

In the months that followed my life and death, I could only say that an envelope opened between the earth and Heaven, and that envelope would remain open in the weeks and months that followed. I felt like I was in an eggshell, and that eggshell cracked, allowing a slit of light to break through from the other side. Even now, daily, that slit of light has remained.

As I noted earlier, I also visited the regions of the dark realm, the second heaven. There I became familiar, in a specific way, with demons and their pitiful state of being and decay. But if I will be perfectly honest, if I were able to lay my eyes upon Heaven again and sit before the throne, I would have liked to stay a bit longer. Well, a lot longer!

During the telling of my miraculous journey, I realize it's a renewed opportunity for you, the reader, to discover a new sense of tranquility that we desperately need in our times. But also, a renewed excitement in your relationship with *the* God of Heaven. All of this takes place in the context of a place of glory and unimaginable beauty.

Sharing my journey with you causes me to think of Paul often and his own experience with the glory. He said that he knows a man who went into the third heaven. Whether it was in spirit or body he could not tell. But beyond a few other words, little information is given.

I get it!

Few words are available to describe the experience when one moves from mortality into immortality. I believe that when Paul stated that he knew a man, that being himself of course, he was no longer that man.

That man is gone.

His former self was no more.

For me as well.

Again, I can close my eyes and squeeze them shut tight as if that will make all of this go away. It doesn't. "So, I dare not be lighthearted in this task of telling others about it," I say to myself.

You see, a process is underway for me too.

Paul had to encounter these feelings.

Of course, you and I have never met, and you don't know me. Ask my wife, children, those in ministry with me, and friends. Ah! They know! They have seen the manifest changes that Paul speaks about. One is changed when you experience the crossing over and being in Heaven, only to return to live again.

In the hours before it all began I didn't realize how severe my physical condition was. A month had passed, you see, in which I was filled with an acute disruption from what doctors called an "internal storm" raging throughout my body. Pain every day. Burning in my midsection that felt like a fiery furnace. All of which was the result of a mistaken overdose in a prescription from my doctor that caused me to ingest seven and a half months of medication in 29 days!

Yes, 29 days!

When taken in such excess, it becomes a toxic cocktail that can lead to a myriad of symptoms like coma, cardiac arrest, and even sudden death. Unbeknownst to me at the time, I was experiencing the preceding symptoms of cardiac arrest. It all intensified for the duration of a full evening, following one month of that inner storm raging. You see, medically, I experienced death, the crossing over.

That fateful evening, I remember trying to convince myself the pain was lessening. I had read and heard many stories of heart attacks and the deep discomfort that precedes them. I told myself repeatedly it would go away, and I continued to focus on staying in the presence of the Lord and reciting His promises.

"If I could just make it through the evening, all would pass, and relief would wash over me with the next sunrise," I thought.

Yet, something else was going on—something deeper.

"Why didn't I suspect more?" I ask myself often to this day. It remains a mystery.

In the early morning hours, at 3 AM when I rose to rest downstairs on the couch trying to remain still, it didn't take long before my heart stopped. In a split second I knew my circle of life had come to an end when my spirit simply and naturally seemed to jump out of my body and began to rise as if I had just completed a night's sleep. I remember going from the physical life to the spiritual in what seemed like a split second.

As my soul began to ascend, I was under a ray of light seemingly beaming from a distant star. That star and light would turn out to be the light of Heaven just ahead of me. It's an immediate realization that comes.

I pause to say that this writing and experience casts me in a light I would rather not see myself in. I am a man who started his life of faith with a very defined picture of who I wanted to be and how I saw myself getting there. I've operated best within the rules or conventional lines for my entire adult life. I have done as I should, whether by guilt, obligation, or just knowing what is right, when the choice was always in question.

I have certainly taken large steps of faith in my life that have come at great cost as well. Faith always comes at a cost. I have also been passionate for the spirit life, always. Yes! Always. With that acknowledgement comes another inevitable, verifiable fact—I don't feel grounded to the earth anymore. A new adventure has begun with a simple declarative taking of all that I have known. So, I press into this writing. I must. Because I am once again recognizing the force behind it.

Often I think to myself, "Perhaps, and only perhaps, I'm playing the part of a driver or guide here," when I recount my experiences of the spiritual realms.

You see, during my telling fantastical places are described for you to pause and consider. You may have no idea which direction to take, but if you jump in as one jumping in a vehicle ready for a journey, I invite you to enjoy the ride. You may find that destination that you are looking for. Why else would I write this book, if it were not for the benefit of your soul, friend?

As the title of the book, *A Rabbi's Journey to Heaven*, implies, deep lessons were taken back, keys to a life of deeper transformation. Upon my return, I was invited to spend 90 days in His glory by the Lord, and for three solid months I would go back and forth, from earth to Heaven. I'm still smiling as I tell anyone and everyone I can about God's miracle. I look to capture anyone's attention who has that deer in the headlights look about their eternal destination.

Friend, with all assurance now I can say that our auspicious end is a magnificent place of glory, with glorious sounds and rhythms. A place of unnatural wonder, where vast miracles are a part of everyday life.

The mountains there are so beautiful. Yes, there are majestic mountains whose heights cannot be fathomed. I am reminded of the psalmist's words in Psalm 65:6, "He establishes mountains by His power," both here and on earth. Angels blow their trumpets from these mountaintops as they are directed by God to ensure the sound carries throughout all the earth, I presume.

So, invite your friends for this telling.

Yes! Invite others.

I was almost home, you see. A place that we will all face at some point in our lives. I must tell you about it, so there is no more groping around in the darkness. Heaven is real, and it is unimaginably wonderful. Hell is real, and it is unimaginably darker than dark. It is darker than black. It is not for you, my friend. I pray that you nod in approval and plunge yourself in the telling of my adventure.

You see, we can press our face into the pillow at night and wonder about what the next day will bring because days come and go quickly. But as quickly as a day comes, it goes. It is the rapidity of life, isn't it, that swallows up the fact that there is another world that we are destined for. We forget that we are travelers on a journey that is always charted inwardly. And therein lies the rub.

1

HEAVEN'S RESIDUE

EXPERIENCING HEAVEN AND THE ETERNAL SPHERES started a systemic, glorious upheaval that has turned my life upside down—or is it right side up? What happens when one's spirit crosses over the divide between Heaven and earth and then returns? A residue has remained. Yes, a residue! I can say that at 68, at the time of this writing, I am no longer fit for the world that I once knew.

I will also admit Bonnie, my dear wife, at times wishes she had her old husband back. I ask Bonnie when she is suddenly overcome with a sweep of anxiety from it all.

"What is it?"

Then, we settle for silence.

In the beginning she had no idea which direction to take. Perhaps she felt like a drowning victim in those last moments of resistance, and reached for the Lord for understanding. She won't allow fear to ever swallow her, because she has always lived strong in the Lord, and she knows that we are both on a new path.

In our life together throughout the years, I built her a house, and she has been the only wonderful woman in that house, and so we have been together for over 45 years. She knows the changes better than anyone. She also remembers the way it was too.

So yes! Changes.

Big changes.

I CAN FLY

First, I feel as if I have just learned how to fly high above the earth. It is what I have imagined in our incorruptible state. Then suddenly, my wings get weighted with something earthly, and I am hurled back to the ground. Being able to have experienced this sense of freedom, when your spirit moves freely through the air, is what occurs when the spirit is no longer confined to the body, or when the corruptible puts on the incorruptible.

You must also know that the spiritual dimension is a parallel universe to this earthly dimension. It's always just beyond us. It's like tasting, feeling, and experiencing something. But this spiritual dimension of existence, is of course, fabulously unearthly and gloriously freeing.

Imagine when your spirit is no longer bound by its earthly and physical limitations. Of course, you are altered forever. The spiritual airways were created for our spirit, or what some call the soul. The difference between the soul and spirit will be explained later in the book.

Now, I am once again confined to my mortal frame, although I live with a daily longing for that immortality again. A moment doesn't pass in a day that I am not aware of its existence. My heart pumps blood throughout my body, my lungs pull in necessary oxygen, but the heavenly experience has become my critical reality in my days on earth.

Let me also say, in the days and months that followed, I wasn't sure that I could make it through another day. It took time to adjust to my soul and spirit feeling somewhat separated.

Peculiar right?

Something happened.

I'm driving my car and I can see myself in the driver's seat from a short distance above. I'm writing this work and I see myself sitting in the chair. I'm speaking to a person, and I can peer into their physical state and discern the kind of person they are:

Are they angry or gentle?

Have they suffered much?

Is faith present in their eyes?

I look into one's eyes and immediately I am immersed into a time tunnel that takes me back to formidable experiences they had as a child.

It seems that when God put me back together, my soul and spirit are no longer tightly compacted together as they once were. An envelope has remained open, or as I mentioned earlier, an eggshell has cracked with a slit of light constantly beaming from the other side. Better said, the veil between the earthly and spiritual has been torn.

Before my experience, I felt like anyone living in a physical body, unconscious of the soul, spirit, and body operating synergistically. I have always seen the body as a vessel that contains the most important part of us—our soul. Even more so now.

Yet this is as unlikely as any fantasy scenario I might ever have created for myself. Instead of viewing myself as a physical being possessing a soul, I recognize myself as a soul temporarily possessing a biological body. Or, a spirit possessing a biological body and soul. They have a symbiotic relationship to one another for the purposes of God's glory.

Strange.

I know.

I have a stronger connection to my spiritual body that has awakened me to a deeper understanding of our divine architecture. Everywhere I go now becomes an adventure.

In my former self, I felt down as anyone from time to time. You know, those times that bring on tightness in the chest, tense shoulders, and altered breathing. We all have them. We can experience anxiety about the current state of our world. That alone can easily bring on an encompassing grip at times.

Now, each day a different universe compels me. There is a lightness or a levity to my physical body, because I feel as though I have been given wings that give me perceptions that can span for miles, or the keen ability to see well beyond my circumstances on any given day. I am always looking beyond my situations to discover new insight that sits behind it.

You should also know that all of my problems haven't been solved or erased, in spite of these blessed effects upon my life. This is because the root cause is as anyone else—living in a fallen world with Satan's handprint everywhere. That is why earth is hard and Heaven is easy.

Certainly, the apostle Paul reveals this throughout his life. Here is a man that was taken into the third heaven, only to return to a load of problems!

Confined to a jail cell (Acts 16:16-40).

Shipwrecked and stranded on an island (Acts 27:15).

Persecuted by his own people (Acts 14:19).

Running from those seeking to stone him.

Imprisoned at the end of his life (Acts 20:22-24).

Finally, beheaded.

Then there is John who was taken into the third heaven, who was given extraordinary visions of the seven churches of Revelation. Yet he remained on the island of Patmos, which was also no paradise.

The third heaven for those who return does not alleviate the earthly difficulties.

As I have begun to adjust back, I have found "safe haven" moments to mitigate the many pressures of earthly life. These are times in a day when I stop to remember that my true home is not here. I look up to the heavens regularly to remember where I was. Then I reset myself again.

Taking such safe-haven moments in a day allows me to string them together throughout a day, week, or month in which I can discover fresh ways to prepare my way forward. I take these moments to appreciate His handiwork everywhere. I stop to listen to people's words so I can understand and learn something in a day. I no longer race throughout my day, because I want to capture all the opportunities.

Friend, I encourage you to look for these safe-haven moments. But you must be intentional. If you stop to listen and observe the world around you, you will find God's handprint everywhere.

More acutely than ever before, I consider daily that to leave this world is to be with Messiah in His glory, and to remain is to be with Him also.

So, what shall I choose?

I am torn now more than ever between the two.

You see, Paul understood how this fabric of life comes under such strain.

> *For what I want to do I do not do, but what I hate I do. ...For I have the desire to do what is good, but I cannot carry it out. For I do not do the good I want to do, but the evil I do not want to do—this I keep on doing* (Romans 7:15,18-19).

I hope my words have pulled on that deep thread within all of us. I see someone reading this who pauses to clear their throat, sighs, and bursts out, "Tell me more!" There is something in all of us of an eternal nature, and we long to understand more of it. It's a mystery imbedded in our souls. This is my vision at least for this writing, hopefully for you as well. So hang on, we're descending deeper!

2

IN A TWINKLING
OF AN EYE

Surely, when thinking of going to our eternal home, no one wants to go too soon. I presume anyone not returning as I did either rises to the glories of Heaven or crash lands in hell. The second is unthinkable. To read about it is one thing, but to experience it and see it is another. Again, the second is unthinkable, because no words are sufficient to describe such an unnecessary circumstance.

For me, it all happened in a twinkling of an eye—it was that fast. The spiritual door swished open, and my last words and actions to Bonnie were a kiss and, *"I'll see you in the morning."* However, the morning never came, at least not the way it normally did.

19

That September morning things spiraled. I was baffled over the feelings in my body. My heart was beating harder, my chest was increasing in pain, increasingly intense burning was running throughout my midsection, and breathing became more intensified.

"In the morning I'll go to the hospital," I thought.

I strove to lay absolutely still throughout the evening, praying that it would go away.

But as I quietly went downstairs at 3 AM to rest, it happened. Within moments after lying down trying to ease the pain, my heart stopped. I guess my heart muscle was tired after a month of that inner storm raging in my body. At a snap of a finger, it was like being shot out of a cannon to a higher plane where life would never be the same.

What. Just. Happened?

My spirit left my body and the crossing over began all in a twinkling of an eye.

Do you know how fast that is?

Eleven one-hundredths of a second. The blinking of an eye is one third of a second. From the spiritual dimension I saw my physical body on the couch where I left it.

Well, here is the point.

I was in the spiritual dimension that fast.

But again, it was not glorious beforehand. *I should have heeded the signs.* Bonnie has finally forgiven me for not calling 911, not waking her up, and not going to the hospital early on.

In sharing my experience with others, some of course shrug and look at me with searching eyes struggling to grasp for some reference. But to no avail. One's experience is one's experience. To another it can seem subjective and not relatable. People mean well, it's just not possible for another to be as immersed. How could they?

There is also this universal fact. A man with an experience is never at the mercy of a man with a theory. One cannot argue with an experience. This seems in the end to always satisfy. You know, yesterday I was blind, today I see. Yesterday I was deaf, today I can hear. I was once bound by the earth, today I am unhinged from it. I only know that in a moment I was before the throne in Heaven. Today I am back on earth.

Nodding. Agreeing. Taking my words for what they are. Readers will understand to the best of their ability. You will too. You see, through my words, it is always God's desire to pull on some thread that will lead you to a larger understanding.

But there are limits.

The apostle Paul understood this, as I reference him often. He states that he *knew* a man, speaking of himself.

Doesn't that leave you on a cliff?

Where is that man?

What happened to him?

But let us return to the twinkling of an eye. In a second or nanosecond I found myself floating in the spiritual dimension while lying horizontally in midair. Truly. My spirit stepped out of my body and it rose up. It had a physical outline and form just like my temporal body. I remember the sensation of being as light as air and feeling like a bird that was just given wings. My spiritual body began to hover in the room slightly below the ceiling, where I could see down at my physical body separated from me. Dead, I presume, lying on the couch.

In the spiritual dimension, I was in a horizontal position, as an angel was standing over my spiritual body. I could not see the angel's face, just a powerful presence and the outline of his figure. His powerful hands were moving over me, but not touching me. There was authority in him that I was keenly aware of.

At the time I could not understand it, but he seemed to be ministering to my soul. I felt like an individual who was just rushed into the emergency room. There was no fear or anxiety, just a deep reassurance and sense of safety washing over me.

I pause from time to time while writing this because my thoughts drift back. I have wondered often why my soul was being ministered to as one who had just arrived in the hospital emergency room. I know that I am repeating myself. But here I am floating in the spiritual realm, my physical body lifeless on the couch, while immersed in a glorious state of bliss and joy, and this angel is over me. Imagine that, this being my death and all.

Apparently, God wants nothing more than our soul to return to Him. It's His love! It's in fact the oldest part of us, you know. All the way back in the Garden when God blew His breath into man, man became a living soul. I now understand why. There is a wonderful life that follows our days on earth. It happens when a wonderful liberation of our soul takes place.

Friend, I am hoping that my words find a seat in your heart and you receive the gift of introspection. Perhaps you will pause for a moment of reflection here.

But something else, too.

"Has God gotten a hold of your soul?"

"Do you believe in God?" No! Not just any God. I mean *the* one who is *the* Creator of Heaven and Earth. You see, while you are alive and breathing, living and filling your lungs with air each day, you don't know when that lightning speed of a second call for eternity will come to you as it did with me.

I didn't know!

In a twinkling of an eye, my breath ceased.

My life expired.

I was merely resting on my couch.

Days and months have passed now. Twelve months, in fact, and I have somehow managed my thoughts. But from time to time, I perch somewhere in a day or a week asking myself, *"That could not have actually happened, right?"*

Certainly, I needed to die and enter into the spiritual dimension to share what I am about to tell you. But I have also returned with a gift that you will receive at the end of this book.

3

LEAVING EARTH BEHIND

My prayer is not that you take them out of the world but that you protect them from the evil one. They are not of the world, even as I am not of it. Sanctify them by the truth; your word is truth (John 17:15-17).

TODAY, I AM HERE LIVING MY LIFE, RELATIVELY obscure, yet I feel like I'm living upon a mountaintop, daily overlooking a grand landscape. My voice is not heard by a thousand ears, yet I live in the presence of a thousand angels.

What I have also found is what I have always known—a beautiful life in His presence brings inner contentment and tranquility, thereby actually prolonging our days here on earth.

You see, many people can live without earthly things and pursuits. Truly, they can. But no one can truly live without the presence of God. It cannot be purchased for any sum of money, but it must be something that comes from the heart and born out of the soul.

As fast as I left, I can relive the events that occurred that September morning in 2019. When I do, the walls of my chest feels like it caves in on itself, and I find it hard to breathe. I feel myself tilt toward Heaven again as if I am being pulled up by an invisible magnet, by a force which I have no power to resist. A sensation returns of what impending death feels like again.

"Is this my new reality?" I ask myself often.

I remember when I rose, I saw my wife Bonnie in the throes of immense grief and sorrow, as she was planning my funeral with my children. In that moment, I saw the future from the spiritual dimension.

I learned that when loved ones depart, they have a momentary awareness of grief and suffering upon those left behind. This offers us some solace knowing that they are aware of how we are suffering.

As I entered the spiritual dimension, there was a white luminous light almost with a blueish hue above me to the right. The light was cylindrical in form and I could see at the end of this funnel-like tunnel. But it was not restrictive, just present. It was a portal. I actually saw many portals where angels were ascending and descending between Heaven and earth during my first three months. It's how ministering angels come to minister to the redeemed of the Lord.

The light, however, was like a blazing fire—no flames, just an intensity surrounding it. Again, it prompted no fear, only an unexplainable peace.

June and September Brought Something Else

You should know that my life-and-death experience was preceded by another set of circumstances. Between June and September, I had already been to Israel twice, and three weeks went by since I was home from my first trip. During my first trip, I had a divine encounter with the Lord at the ancient Wailing Wall, only to return knowing that something had happened to me.

When I returned, I couldn't sleep or resume life as usual. For some unknown reason I was compelled to return, "But for what?" I thought.

Finally, Bonnie said, "All right, but you need to assure me that if you go, you'll find what God wants."

"I'm only doing it to verify the inner witness that is screaming loudly right now," I explained to her.

But as she has always done, she nodded with that look, "I understand."

I know she wished I had a more affirmative response, but that is the way it was.

Only three weeks passed and I was back in Jerusalem spending seven days in prayer at the Wailing Wall, seeking the Lord at prayer houses, and in deep meditation at the Tower of David. Thankfully, resolution finally came, and I knew that I completed an assignment, even though I didn't understand its full purpose yet. Perhaps it was a test of obedience for obedience's sake! Perhaps it was preparation for what I was about to go through.

You never know at the time.

You just do it and obey.

I'M FINALLY HOME

After arriving home with that deep resolve, something began to feel acutely wrong. I had gone to the doctor for my regular exam and everything seemed fine. But I began to feel out of sorts in my body. It seemed to descend into a base of nervousness and unrest. I didn't know at the time that my body was undergoing the early signs of the internal storm that I mentioned earlier from the doctor's error, or that it was a clue of impending death.

A solid month went by. Every day I felt as if I was groping around the darkness, confused, deeply disturbed within my body. But one catastrophic morning at 3 AM, my body finally said enough. My heart stopped, and my spiritual journey to the spiritual frontier began.

In the glorious months that followed, I was here physically, but in my spirit I was detached. That still lingers. You will understand as you journey with me. I felt born again, again. I felt like a newborn nursing on the presence of Heaven taking in every drop of heavenly milk, figuratively speaking of course.

Factually, I was literally drawn into a fetal position in the shower every morning for three months, weeping, receiving, and experiencing. That's the way it was! Of course, Bonnie and my children had to deal with a new set of changes again. But Bonnie knew that I was never known to have an overactive imagination either. So I would often nod, then think a moment only to say, "This is something new."

Everything is incapable of fitting in now. It's like trying to put a round peg in a square hole. And I am sure that others who have been shot out of that same spiritual cannon have confronted the same disadvantages, as well as advantages.

If it should happen to you, my dear reader, my words will resound in your heart and mind. You will be forever changed by a tsunami of heavenly forces—the eternal spheres, the places where angels fly, where the throne of the Almighty resides. One day you're bound by the earth. Mortal. Confined. The next moment you're free. Immortal. Only to surrender to mortality again.

GIVEN A CHOICE

More than twelve months have passed now, and the spinning has slowed. My days have stabilized. Yet one fact remains—I knew I had a choice at the time. This is really important. It was whether it will be transformational or transactional. These two choices are always presented in times of holy visitations, or when the miraculous comes knocking upon the door of your life.

Which one will you choose?

You see, with God, I have always wanted the full ride, because it is really an adventurous life with God. So your choice makes all the difference.

I must explain more.

We don't realize it at the time, but when we are basking in the experience of a revival, perhaps, or any move of God, or a miracle similar to what I experienced, these two choices are both precarious and life altering.

Precarious because *transactional* ends up being experiential. Over time you find yourself back in your old self. No changes took hold. *Transformational* radically alters things. You are willing to pay the price for the lasting change, and nothing will be the same ever again. But it also takes intentionality and forcefulness to maintain the transformation. It's like vowing something to the Lord and holding tightly to it.

God spoke to my heart and said that He would require a greater discipline in my life to maintain what He had given me. That this miraculous second chance at life would have far more reaching consequences than I would ever imagine. Because I said, "Yes, I'm ready for that drink."

THE COST

I first understood that it meant living quieter with less activity and observing and listening more. I needed to be ready in and out of season to respond to His commands. Living more detached from this world was a key. We know that we are not of this world. Isn't this what Yeshua tells us in John 16:16?

Yes! These deeper transformations come at a price! Now looking back, I made the right choice as I did in the years of revival. We determined to never go back that day when Bonnie and I raised our hands to the Lord as a wave offering to say yes! Lord, take us!

4

HEAVEN'S PERCEPTIONS

However, as it is written: "What no eye has seen, what no ear has heard, and what no human mind has conceived"—the things God has prepared for those who love him (1 Corinthians 2:9).

THROUGHOUT THE FIRST TWELVE MONTHS, AND WHAT began with a greater intensity in the first three, I returned with a complex of new sensations and perceptions, new routines, and each day I am living a more glory-centered life. Like the fragrance that remains after the flower is gone, Heaven has left its scent everywhere now.

Nothing has affected me more, though, than when I saw the Lord sitting upon His throne high and lifted up above the crystal sea. The throne was close enough for me that no thoughts could come to mind, only deep reverential fear drowning me in an unexplainable grand reverence.

The details of His hands and feet were lifelike, except His face was veiled. I could only see a frame, which was obscured by a glorious light and fire that surrounded Him and the throne. It all caused my head to bow lower and lower from the knee down until I lay prostrate before Him.

The legs of the throne touched the crystal firmament. His throne was surrounded by a ring of fire. My eyes needed to be shielded from its light, and even to this day, I must cover my eyes when I go into His presence.

Throughout Heaven, there were streets of gold everywhere. Golden walkways were filled with the redeemed, gloriously and peacefully walking together in white raiment. They were talking with each other, and although I could not determine what they were saying, their voices sounded like a multitude of voices upon a sea of redeemed.

What was extraordinary was how they spoke to one another in a firm yet gentle whisper, and there was a sense of assurance and finality in their voices.

Why? I presume because they were home and finally clothed in their incorruptible self.

Perfection. Completion.

Oh yes! I can say there is activity in Heaven, friend!

Glorious activity.

If you have lost a loved one who knew the Lord, you would be overwhelmed by an open floodgate of happiness. A wellspring of joy. If you could only see them in their glorious state.

Contrary to our earthly knowledge, one that is laced with intense emotion, they do not feel sadness, but only a sense of divine peace and a full knowledge. They know fully what we see and know in part. Theirs is an unexplainable tranquility that is not attainable as earthlings. I know this because I briefly experienced it. So our challenge as earthlings is to free our loved ones into the fullness of what the Lord has prepared for them.

Yes! It's not easy.

But this is true love, isn't?

To do so is perhaps a foretaste of perfect love.

Yes! Perfection again.

Listening to the tone of their voices, I was reminded of when the Lord's audible voice came to me at 3 AM in the morning over two decades ago. He spoke into my left ear and said: "I am bringing you back to your people." It too was deep, commanding, quiet like a whisper, but firm and commanding, and strangely it also took place at 3 AM.

So yes, at 68 years old, new perspectives are before me daily. I no longer know what I used to know because everything is different. The air is quiet, and my mind is filled with a heavenly record of my visit.

Although every morning arrives as it did before, often around 3 AM, when my heart stopped, I am drawn downstairs out of my sleep to be with God—it's an appointment that begins routinely. I whisper to Bonnie on my left, "It's time, I have to go up," and she knows what that means. Sometimes she falls back asleep, or other times she begins her own prayer time. At least a couple of hours pass, and no sooner is it dawn, and I hear a stir from the second floor. She steps into the room, and we both share and soak up each other's words. It doesn't happen every morning, I assure you. But when it does, we're both imprinted with something beautiful and heavenly. Then, often with labored breathing, I enter the weight of His presence. My inside burns and I have fire in my belly again, but this time from a different source.

WALKING IN THE SPIRITUAL DIMENSION

At the moment of separation and the crossing over, the spirit is outside of the body. I felt like I was in some place between the second and third heaven at first. But that cylindrical light-like tunnel, the light of Heaven, always hovered high up toward the right of me.

This spiritual dimension is as real as this earthly realm but of a non-earthly material, and I realized it's what we were created for. The Bible calls it the incorruptible realm

(1 Corinthians 15:53). The apostle Paul describes his ascending to Heaven in 2 Corinthians 12:2, *"I know a man in Christ who fourteen years ago was caught up to the third heaven. Whether it was in the body or out of the body I do not know—God knows."*

He had to have seen the same river I saw as clear as crystal—one whose origin and end I could not see. As previously noted, mountains so majestic and high that their peaks could not be determined.

I said earlier that angels blow their trumpets from these mountains. I saw one blow their trumpet in November of 2019 over the earth to announce that a time of fear, panic, and trembling will be released upon the continents of the earth, which would come to be COVID-19.

So shaken was I by the vision that I could not absorb any more. I asked the Lord if I could return in the morning at the same time at 3 AM. In the morning I came back at 3 AM for the second half of the vision, which would take place on a third day as well.

Heaven: The Ultimate Showplace

Oh! What a glorious place! Heaven is the ultimate showplace of God's divine creativity. Imagine everything and everyone on earth untouched by human hands. Untainted by humanity. I think of the Garden of Eden before the fall. Well, this is Heaven! Yes! Untainted humanity just like it was in the Garden of Eden before the fall.

Paul had to have seen this Heaven that I saw, with its foundation of pearl held in place like a jeweler's stone within a glorious frame. Truly! Streets lined with gold and pearl throughout, the most beautiful sunrises and sunsets pale in comparison.

Heaven's gates said, "Righteousness and Justice," and all those who enter through these gates enter a world of righteousness and justice. Truth and righteousness are the permanent order of things in the Holy City.

There is no night, of course, because everything and everyone is sustained by His glory, which is light. I felt free from the natural sustaining elements such as sleep, food, and water, because it is an entirely self-sustainable place and designed for the incorruptible saints and angels. Imagine living in a blissful, glory-filled atmosphere that is sparkling with gold flecks. That's the way it was.

It reminded me of when our congregation went through revival over twenty years ago, when Sabbaths were filled with the youth experiencing gold dust. Several times they went home covered in it. Gold dust was everywhere. I guess it was rain from Heaven. Now from the brightness of His glory in Heaven, I find myself on earth covering my eyes when going into the presence of God.

You see, I saw the shadow of the feet of our Messiah and His footstool pressed and resting on the sea of glass that separated the earthly realm from the heavenly. It was reassuring because God can see everything.

He sees you wherever you are.

He sees you as you are on this journey with me.

His eyes are like an eagle, able to descend upon the tiniest subject of interest.

Have your spiritual senses come alive yet, friend? Mine will forever be emboldened until I return again.

5

HEAVEN'S DAILY CHANGES

WELL, NEVER COULD I IMAGINE THAT I WOULD HAVE such an experience in my life. Now I know that nothing that anyone could imagine or conceive of in their mind comes close.

In Heaven I saw an endless border of seamless glory from one end to the other. Streams of water running as clear as crystal flowing throughout. It followed a path back toward the area of the throne, where a grand river was. Its water appeared as the deepest blue, yet transparent. I saw the redeemed dressed in white standing along that riverbed.

Mountains ascended upward into a canopy of blue displaying all the colors of the rainbow, yet cast in a shimmering iridescent. God's throne was never far away because it had an imposing but arresting presence on all. It was manifest everywhere. God's presence was stamped on everything and everyone.

As noted earlier, the throne was encircled by a golden majesty of deep, swirling fire. I am perhaps repeating myself here only to imprint your mind with a picture of a light so bright that I needed to shield my eyes from its brilliance. But for the redeemed, they seemed to be able to withstand more of its intensity. This is not to say that they didn't bow or behave deeply reverent before the throne.

No!

Heavens, no!

Reverential fear of God was everywhere. But I assumed it was due to their permanent eternal state that they could tolerate more light. Perhaps because I was only visiting and destined to return, my eyes could only behold a lesser brilliance than them.

Heaven is also a place of continuous music, worship, and choruses. The redeemed along with the angels worship day in and day out. I have days now when I hear angels' voices coming from the spiritual realms. I learned that when we join in one voice giving glory to God in corporate worship, we form a continuum of one orchestra of voices.

I mention this often, but gold is everywhere. Gemstones sparkle from riverbeds brilliantly embellishing God's glory. Their brilliance was more vibrant and richer than the purest gold or precious stones that have ever passed through my hands. All of this holds special significance to me.

You see, for two decades before full-time service to God, my secular work was in the area of precious metals and stones. I dealt with the most valuable of diamonds, rubies, and pearls. In my hands I held pure gold bars weighing 400 ounces. So I know pure gold, precious stones, and silver when I see it. Heaven's precious metals and stones were unsurpassed by anything on earth.

The sea! Oh! There was a great crystal sea that appeared like glass whose unimaginable borders shone and sparkled like gold and diamonds. Above the sea was a heavenly canopy of blue far more beautiful than the lapis lazuli, amethyst, or blue sapphire that I was familiar with in my working days.

FREEDOM

Freedom!

Finally!

I was untethered from my physical body, you see—finally detached. I can only imagine what a new bird must feel the first time it learns to fly. I arrived to fulfill my purpose—be free! I learned that as it's instinctive for them, it's spiritually instinctive for us. It's what we are all destined for.

As my soul experienced freedom from the confines of the earth, I had the privilege of experiencing a snippet of immortality. To this day, the winds on any given day compel me to stretch out my hands into the wind, to allow the wind to flow through them.

Is the wind a connection to immortality that I sensed?

To some degree, yes! It's the freedom of the wind with its unharnessed jaunt through the airways that I connect to.

Yes! I believe so.

But it is yet a mystery!

Someday, gloriously, it will happen to all of God's children (1 Corinthians 15).

I take moments to pause for a deep breath in the midst of this writing, realizing that there were times when I wanted my former life back. You see, there was a time when I could not see how my life is going to fit anything anymore. But now I know that I have been given a gift, and I don't ever want to go back. I live feeling excised from the earth in part, and it is liberating.

SENSES ARE HEIGHTENED

Master of my senses!

Yes!

Something happened to my five senses upon my return. I see and hear more acutely. Insignificant things once overlooked are magnified. A caterpillar, a fly, or the smallest of creatures. I notice how an ant is packed with divine design. I take notice of the various birds of the air that take flight upon a God-given wind. Yet they know not their maker. Only a God-given instinct drives them from the nest to the air to their last resting place. Take the sparrow, the hawk, and the eagle. All three were given wings to fly. Yet when they take flight, their activities are as different as night and day.

My taste buds have been altered. For reasons only known to my Father, my desire for coffee left me like the morning mist and has not returned. Spicy foods once intolerable are now enjoyable. I eat simpler and cleaner because I have a verifiable sense that God wants my body cleaner, healthier, and stronger.

I cannot indulge myself in the few things that I once enjoyed. Certainly, over the course of my life, the indulgences of my youth are long gone. But the one holdout I could say was coffee! I did love my morning coffee and the aroma that would fill the morning hours.

Details are seen as never before!

I've become aware of colors, textures, the distances around me. Every nuance of a tree's bark, a leaf blowing in the wind, a love song performed by a bird in the springtime—all captures my attention.

I like to walk in the rain, stand in the middle of the street on a windy day, and lift my hands to the heavens to feel its power. Not as individuals who worship nature or through New Age thoughts, but as one who gives all glory and honor to our God, who is the Creator of everything.

My health was also affected.

Following a battery of tests in the months that followed to ensure that my organs had not been damaged by the intense dosage of medication, the doctors were confounded to report that my blood work was like a young person. It seems perhaps that at 68, just maybe, God has lengthened my days.

Every day is a like turning the page in my own storybook adventure. I never want this to leave!

Who has done this?

God our Creator!

You see, there is no room for boredom. The world seems smaller than ever now, because there is a new but familiar wonderland to explore far larger. Mainly because the spiritual realm is larger and boundless. As you become subject to a greater spiritual invasion, you notice God's handprint almost everywhere.

WALKS EVERY DAY

"Sir, look up to the sky, isn't that blue magnificent?" I say often to a casual stroller on his walk in the morning.

The outside has become one of my sacred spaces where I engage anyone I can to make known the mighty deeds of the Lord. Often in the face of the morning sunrise I kneel down on the sidewalk along the road to lift my hands to worship Him, caring little for appearances.

So I feel called outside to look up into the heavens where I visited and give thanks to my God. The psalmist states in chapter 68 verse 34, "Whose power is in the heavens." You see, there is a sense of greater freedom there for me in this season.

It's more space.

It orients me to the heavens, where my Master's voice is sent out upon the earth. From north to south and east to west, there's nowhere His voice can't be heard. His power is ascribed about us daily.

God's people should pause in a day to consider the work of His hands. I understand the words of the psalmist when he writes, *"Great are the works of the Lord; they are pondered by all who delight in them"* (Psalm 111:2). And now I have become a student of His handiwork.

In the evenings I step outside to take great deep breaths, while gazing into the night sky marveling at the starry heaven. It's all for us, friend! We can look around and receive what nature teaches us. These are the many wonders of God. His laws are masterpieces that keep harmony in all of its parts.

Stop. Look. Listen.

AVERSION TO ALL VIOLENCE

More than ever before, I direct my attention away from all violence. The idea of hunting and killing an animal becomes repugnant. Killing, violence, abuse, and aggressiveness are such things that deliver a stronger aversion than ever before. The spirit churns within me when I see the levels of prejudice and bigotry today.

The image of injustice on Black Americans is intolerable. White arrogance and supremacy are a disdain. The injustices levied against the helpless, the poor, the weak, and the wanderer, who does not have a home to call his own. Also repugnant is the apathy of the church, its arrogance and self-sufficiency, and the hungry at her doorstep. She is blind to her own spiritual condition.

You see, my friend, it's all about the scepter of righteousness of the Kingdom. When each and every one of us bow before that, the pain of seeing the injustices, hypocrisies, and selfishness in our land will be felt more and more by all. Stop. Look. Listen.

BEING AN OBSERVER

At times, I have a desire to be the old man by the sea sitting in a beach chair in the shade of a thatched roof, watching and observing everything. Living more as an observer every day, I take notice of people's activities, position, and authority. King Solomon was a master observer. I am only a student in comparison. Something may have happened in his life that birthed a realization of the world around him. I get it!

Potentially upsetting situations, I step away from— not literally but emotionally. You see, God created us with the power of choice not to respond or, yes, retaliate. We can feel good even in the mist of nasty or cruel people. I detach. This is something that I speak more about later in the book.

I marvel at the fact that everyone has been given a divine activity under the sun, and that activity fills the hours, days, months, and years of one's life. But I also realize many are trapped in a work where man becomes diverted from the adoration of our Father in Heaven. We can be like ants working collectively without rest, spending our lives in a relentless pattern of work. Round and round, work whirls around us as a force of nature.

It cries out, never enough!

It wants more!

Never is it satisfied!

It comes from our own relentless pursuits layered with our self-imposed pressures. We strive for importance, position, power, and the praise of man. But all of it has no value upon our eternity. Scientific studies have shown that in any given day we can make 35,000 choices, which is 12,775,000 choices in a year. Of those choices, how many have chosen to stop to observe the handiwork of our Creator, or to stop and worship and adore our God?

All of these forces are the wild driving forces within man that are untamed by Heaven. I call it the "call of the wild." Now, I shut down the call of the wild for the gentle breeze that carries my Father's messages in a day. By His Spirit, I hear better, see better, understand more, want more, and strive for higher planes.

The fact is, we squander years only to come to the end of our lives, wishing we would have, could have, and should have spent more time on the things that truly mattered.

COVID-19 should have awakened many to the fragility of life, including the rapidity of our days. The psalmist reminds us that God knows our frame. He remembers that we are merely dust (Psalm 103:14). What do you want for your life, friend?

UN-POLITICIZED

Another extraordinary change is that I have returned completely untouched by the hot political environment of our times. I realized I could not afford to be politically motivated or favor one side or the other as new prophetic streams are flowing within me. Prophetic ministry must be objective, untouched by presumption, which has been evident in our present time.

One of my earliest lessons in the clear black of all the confusion was the new level of persuasion of the Kingdom. It felt like an iron anvil falling from the sky crushing the governments of man. The scepter of His Kingdom came powerfully. Now to a greater degree, I follow the Kingdom and its constitution, the Word of God, and its laws. I am consumed with it. I feel I'm one with it. I put on my spiritual running shoes daily to go after it like a runner headed for the finish line.

I do listen now and then to man's speeches, but let me suggest that you let their words stand on their own without your preconceived ideas, presumptions, and political affiliations.

Do their words have legs to stand on?

Are they merely words that fly away into the air?

Are their character and actions married to their words? Likely, while listening to many today, you will feel the instant horror of most of their words and immediately pray, "Lord, let Your kingdom come." That's what Daniel wanted. It's what we all want.

GUIDES IN MY LIFE

In my new life, I have come to appreciate the spiritual guides or guideposts in my life. New Age philosophies also use the word *guides*, but this is one of those many reclamations that I make in my life that was stolen by humanism and the occult.

Let me explain.

In the Bible there are spiritual guides. In 1 Corinthians 4:15 Paul states: *"For though you have countless guides in*

Christ, you do not have many fathers. For I became your father in Christ Jesus through the gospel" (ESV). A guide in New Testament times was applied to trustworthy men who were charged with the duty of supervising the life and morals of boys before the age of manhood.

In James 3:3, it states the following with a slightly different meaning: *"If we put bits into the mouths of horses so that they obey us, we guide their whole bodies as well"* (ESV). The word *guide* here refers to impartation of some absolute truth.

The New Age use of the word *guide* is parallel to what Isaiah states: *"O my people, your guides mislead you and they have swallowed up the course of your paths* (Isaiah 3:12 ESV). Then from Yeshua, *"Every plant that my heavenly Father has not planted will be pulled up by the roots. Leave them; they are blind guides. If the blind lead the blind, both will fall into a pit"* (Matthew 15:14).

Hence, I esteem the following guides: The Holy Spirit, the Bible, prayer, exaltation, divine appointments, men of God, prophets, teachers, counselors, pastors, apostles, evangelists. I esteem men whose lives are quiet as the woods, but when they speak, they speak of things that they know.

FEARLESSNESS

I have returned with a profound absence of fear, yet I have never struggled with it before my experience. There is no fear of death, sickness, disease, the everyday uncertainties of life, or what political party is ruling, or what dire predictions are made. There is internal respect for dangers, because I know that my actions have consequences. But my life flow fearlessly transcends what transpires in a day or a season.

Because my soul experienced its passing once, I can sense Heaven's call will one day call again, but its prospect holds no sadness or dread. The re-gifting of my life reshaped the old constructs, you see. It has expanded my earthly existence into a higher realm. I live in the moment and allow the daily flow to carry me unfettered by concerns of tomorrow.

> *Therefore I tell you, do not worry about your life, what you will eat or drink; or about your body, what you will wear. Is not life more than food, and the body more than clothes? Look at the birds of the air; they do not sow or reap or store away in barns, and yet your heavenly Father feeds them. Are you not much more valuable than they? Can any one of you by worrying add a single hour to your life?* (Matthew 6:25-27)

> *There is no fear in love. But perfect love drives out fear, because fear has to do with punishment. The one who fears is not made perfect in love* (1 John 4:18).

6

WHAT I LEARNED ABOUT SPIRITUAL WARFARE

ALTHOUGH THIS WORLD IS NOT A PLACE WHERE WE ARE to be always, Satan is authenticated through real spiritual warfare in a believer's life (2 Thessalonians 2:18; 2 Corinthians 2:11). Here there is no disagreement.

But one afternoon God invited me into the second heaven where demons reside. I was standing upon a firmament separating the second heaven, or the lower firmament, from the upper airways. It was a barrier that demons could not cross or climb over, because it is where they have been consigned. In other words, they cannot enter the upper airways where the people of God inhabit. I stress again that I am speaking only of children of God who are covered in the blood of Yeshua. I am not referring to the unsaved.

But my long-held theology would be upset once again.

One particular demon (and I noticed hordes of them) desperately tried to reach up and take hold of my ankles. Pitifully and powerlessly, it had no ability to enter my airspace, as his attempts were futile, which frustrated the demon. I contemplated this only to realize what I have always known but have never witnessed before.

Paul writes that *unbelievers* are caught in the snares of the devil (2 Timothy 2:26). In another area he states, *"In their case the god of this world has blinded the minds of the unbelievers, to keep them from seeing the light of the gospel of the glory of Christ, who is the image of God"* (2 Corinthians 4:4 ESV). Then these words: *"In which you once walked, following the course of this world, following the prince of the power of the air, the spirit that is now at work in the **sons of disobedience**"* (Ephesians 2:2 ESV).

We who are the redeemed, however, the "sons of obedience," are no longer under the rule of Satan or his demonic horde. Colossians 1:13-14 states, *"He has delivered us from the domain of darkness and transferred us to the kingdom of his beloved Son, in whom we have redemption, the forgiveness of sins"* (ESV).

This domain of darkness is not only the shadow of death that we have been freed from but the entire sphere of Satan. It is the blood of Yeshua and the kingdom of light that took dominion over the work of darkness in our lives.

You see, we're sealed by the blood of Yeshua. It actually antagonizes and frustrates them. Slithering beings, they have no choice but to serve their master of darkness. When the Bible indicates that our adversary is the god of this world, he is, but it does not mean that he was given ultimate authority. No! Rather, he rules over the unbelieving world in a specific way. Let me take you further.

CONSIGNED TO THE LOWER REALM

Although Satan is the prince of the power of the air, (Ephesians 2:2) and ruler of the world (John 12:31), understand this very important point—he moves and reigns in the lower airways below our feet, because we are the children of God. It occurred to me while over the second heaven that a child of God can freely raise their hands to Heaven and proclaim His promises because our hands and words of our lips are unfettered by demonic resistance—it's our domain because we are covered by His blood. He has already moved us out of the kingdom of darkness.

In other words, we have all authority from our feet, or let me say, from the ground up, and all the way up to the heavens. Yet my suspicion is the so-called demons are running their own manhunt for God's people through their preoccupation with demons and demonology. I see this fact fit my suspicion in many lives over the course of ministry.

But you might ask, what and who are these demons? Demons are fallen angels who lost the physical and spiritual attributes they had when they were first created by God. Following their fall, they began to deteriorate and become ugly, and I saw how awful and dreadfully deformed they were. As we go from life to life, they go from death unto death in a systematic decay. They are pitiful because they have no power over us, yet they try repeatedly.

You see, like their master, they are in a spirit of delusion. They tried repeatedly to climb up to reach for my ankles or find any hold they could, but they could not break through the lower firmament where they were consigned. It clearly states in Genesis 3:14, "The Lord God said to the serpent, '*Because you have done this, cursed are you above all livestock and all wild animals! You will crawl on your belly and you will eat dust all the days of your life.*'"

SOURCE OF OUR DIFFICULTIES

What then is the source of our difficulties? On earth, we will never completely purge our life of difficulties; it's a daily resistance, or the rub of two kingdoms against each other. This is because the world remains dominated by the prince of darkness. Everything is tainted by the fall.

Repeating what was been stated in an earlier chapter: All of my problems haven't been solved, nor erased in lieu of my extraordinary journey.

Why? It's the rub! Earthly life is hard and Heaven is easy. Consider how much our forefathers of faith had to bear up before they were finally allowed to set one foot upon the beautiful Promised Land.

Remember the apostle Paul's difficulties in spite of being taken into the third heaven. Let's review them again. In his life he was confined to a jail cell (Acts 16:16-40), shipwrecked, stranded on an island (Acts 27:15), persecuted by his own people (Acts 14:19), and constantly running from those seeking to stone him; then he was imprisoned toward the end of his life (Acts 20:22-24).

We learn that the road from the earth to the Promised Land is often not a straight or short one. I am certain that you can attest to this. Life can be a hard, winding road filled with dangers, trials, and tribulations. Often, we must pass through the wildernesses of pain, suffering, and loss. God often takes us by roundabout and indirect means. None of this was a demonic intrusion from within, but an outside world that is fallen, the obtrusive evil nature of unredeemed man that we encounter daily in our life.

God is also sovereign and allows things to be sifted through His hands for our good. He chose not to lead the Israelites in a direct line straight from Egypt to Canaan, but 200 hundred miles around. Then He made them occupy desert wanderings for forty years, only to bring them into Canaan on the side furthest from Egypt. So it is with God, and so it is with our life as God's people.

God will have us live on bread, but He does not make the bread for us. No! God creates the plant and leaves it to be nourished by the air and water to finally ripen so that it bears that beautiful golden grain to make bread to eat.

God's way is to allow His children time to gather their experiences in life so they can learn to throw off habits that bind them. Many times, we must live under greater discipline to learn the art of war, so to gain a steadiness and courage in the face of our enemies in the greater calling to come.

Finally, all of us, you see, are born into a certain sphere, with certain powers. Then God allows the circumstances of life to work within us. This takes place under divine supervision. Not that it hasn't occurred to you, but Yeshua Himself did not enter into His ministry at once, but remained in obscurity for thirty years before His mission began. Moses was fit only after so many things had befallen him. He underwent training for 80 years. Then there are those difficulties inherent in life as noted above. But all of this is not a direct attack or assignment of Satan and his cohorts.

THE TONGUE HOLDS THE POWER
OF LIFE AND DEATH

In my newfound understanding I was also challenged by a familiar passage that I have always used and memorized: *"The tongue has the power of life and death"* (Proverbs

18:21). For weeks I pondered this passage. My conclusion may bring the sharpest of disagreement, but this passage is so often misquoted and taken grossly out of context.

One of the most common teachings on this passage is that the devil can respond to our words, because he can hear us and then attack us. As a matter of fact, the idea behind this is by no means new.

In the basic presupposition, if one speaks of disease one can be waylaid by the enemy with an attack of sickness. Such teaching proves nothing. Satan and his cohorts do not have that power! Remember? If one reads the context a truer translation is as follows: "Many a one has caused his own death, or the death of others, by a false or injurious tongue."

Proverbs 18:21 has everything to do with our behavior, reactions, and speech. It deals with a certain manner of living that can invite problems when our mind and tongue are driven by a chariot of wild horses.

Surely, God's people are not these defenseless, weak lambs who must live fearfully from diverse kinds of attacks because of a word or conversation that falls from our lips.

You see, my friend, I no longer live under a ceiling but an open sky. I choose the open sky and a limitless, free life, because the blood of Messiah is all sufficient against the works of darkness as we have demonstrated earlier.

Let me also say, I do not speak about sickness and disease, *ever*. I maintain a proper thought life, which is rooted in the provision of divine health and healing. Nor do I speak of depression or sadness. I maintain a healthy thought life so my soul is healthy.

CONCLUSION

As many difficult circumstances come to us, we live in our mortal frames traveling through a world still dominated by this prince of the power of the air. The world will remain under its influence until our King of kings returns. Then it will be transformed and renewed.

Hence, we will pass through many wilderness tests, but we will find God's guidance—His pillar of fire by night and the cloud by day, figuratively speaking. This teaches us this fine moral.

Let's *stop* consigning blame for our difficulties on Satan or the demons. God is far more involved in our life than we think, and Satan is far less involved in our life than we think. When we consign the cause of our problems to an adversary that is powerless, we render the power of Messiah's testimony impotent when He is, in fact, *all powerful!*

7

SOUL AND SPIRIT

So I say, walk by the Spirit, and you will not gratify the desires of the flesh. For the flesh desires what is contrary to the Spirit, and the Spirit what is contrary to the flesh. They are in conflict with each other, so that you are not to do whatever you want (Galatians 5:16-17).

OUT OF THE DUST

Following my encounter, the Lord began to unfold the mysteries between my soul and spirit, and how they're connected. In the past that was information that was not particularly needed.

I was imprinted with a new curiosity ever since that spiritual envelope remained open. But was it my soul that left my body or was it my spirit? They can look alike to each other, and are often synonymous with one another. So the first thing I did was to have a look in the Scriptures.

Journey with me, then, and let's take a look.

Immortality, what I briefly experienced, focuses upon the destiny of the soul—or is it the spirit? In other words, which part goes to Heaven and which part remains? Either man's soul departs or his spirit departs, because in Hebrew *ruach* means spirit and *nefesh* means soul.

I found it to be a topic that is often met with confusion, and it wasn't long before I began to realize that soul and spirit are used interchangeably by the authors of the Bible.

In one such passage Yeshua says, *"Now my soul is troubled"* (John 12:27). In the very next chapter, I noticed that Yeshua was *"troubled in spirit"* (John 13:21). Then in Luke 1:46-47, *"My soul glorifies the Lord, and my spirit rejoices in God my Savior."* Those words stayed with me.

Surely, the soul is the part of man that includes his intellect, his emotions, and his will. In the Greek, it is *psyche*, where we get the word *psychology*, and in Hebrew it is *nefesh*, meaning soul. So we can readily see how it influences our lives.

But the spirit is different.

The spirit is the higher order of a person. It comes alive unto God's purposes when one becomes a believer in the Messiah, then the unredeemed spirit comes alive (Romans 8:10).

Proverbs 16:32 speaks of one "who rules his spirit" (NKJV), implying that both the soul and spirit can sin. Here the soul can do everything the spirit can, and the spirit can do everything the soul can. So for good reason, soul and spirit are used interchangeably and are met with some confusion.

My own out-of-body encounter taught me that the spirit carries many of the same attributes of our physical soul. This requires some explanation.

The spirit is not some mystical mist or of an inanimate nature. It was created by God to give life to a living soul. When my spirit rose out of my body and hovered in the room, I could see my physical body. In that moment, I understood it was dead, so the spirit, or the immortal body, can see as I saw in Heaven. It also has intelligence, sight, passion, and emotion.

For instance, in Heaven the spirits of the redeemed worship God continually with great exuberance, i.e. emotion. The spirit can also see prophetically, because I saw into the future when Bonnie was planning my funeral.

Hence, the spirit carries familiar attributes as when we are in the physical realm. The difference is that those attributes are fully redeemed and flawless when we put on immortality. So man's spirit is the part of him that is most often connected to his relationship to God; the spirit directs his soul to worship and pray to God (Psalm 103:1; John 4:24; Philippians 3:3).

Remember! God breathed the breath of life into his nostrils, and man became a living soul.

I shifted my attention to other writings in the Bible, where we see that people who have died and gone to Heaven or hell are referred to as both "spirits" or "souls" (Revelation 6:9; 20:4; 1 Peter 3:19). Rachel's death is described: *"her soul was departing (for she died)"* (Genesis 35:18 NKJV).

Elijah prayed for a dead child that his soul would return to him (1 Kings 17:21). Isaiah spoke about the servant of the Lord who would pour out his soul to death (Isaiah 53:12). Finally, in Luke 12:20 God says, *"Fool! This night your soul is required of you, and the things you have prepared, whose will they be?"* (ESV).

In the Bible we see the spirit ascending and returning to God at the point of death (Psalm 31:5; Luke 23:46; John 19:30; Ecclesiastes 12). When Yeshua was dying, He bowed his head and gave up his spirit (John 19:30), as did Stephen (Acts 7:59). Yet in another place, Yeshua told us not to fear those who "kill the body but cannot kill the *soul*," but that we should rather *"fear him who can destroy both soul and body in hell"* (Matthew 10:28 ESV).

The *soul* here refers to the part of a person that exists after death. How can one kill the body and not the person? One is speaking of a man who has power only over the body. Satan, on the other hand, has the power to take the whole person to hell.

So when Yeshua speaks about *"soul* and body," he is clearly referring to the entire person even though he does not mention spirit as a separate component. Repeatedly, the word *soul* seems to stand for the entire nonphysical part of man. But it is the spirit that returns to Heaven as mine did.

NEFESH HA CHAIM: LIVING SOUL

I want to now introduce you to a Hebrew term, *Nefesh Ha Chaim,* or the living *soul.* I want to break it down into three parts in such a way that no outward knowledge can give. It is illustrated as follows:

The *soul* is likened to the breath of air that a glassblower uses to inflate hot glass. The first is the air that is still in the glassblower's cheeks. This is corresponding to the *neshama* (soul), the part of man which is most connected to God. Notice, God has not released the air yet.

But when the air leaves the glassblower's mouth and flows down a tube, the tube connects the glassblower and his work—that is God to man and soul to God. This flow of wind is the *ruach!*

Again, from a tube, the air enters the glass, like "dust of the ground" as referenced back in Genesis. This then becomes the *nefesh*, or life-giving *soul*, and the purpose of our physical selves.

This means that the *soul* and body are not the same thing. The body derives its origin from the earth, the soil, or the dust. Soul, it is said, is God breathed into the nostrils and thus becomes the breath of life. Then divine breath expanded the lungs and transformed a man into a living being, or a living soul. This made us into a spiritual being with a capacity for serving and fellowshipping with God. Yet the Spirit lives beyond the body and the grave.

In conclusion, the authors of the Bible were unconcerned if they said the soul departs or the spirit departs. To them it seemed they meant the same thing. The soul and spirit are found to be general terms to describe the immaterial side of a man, and often the difficulty is in seeing any real distinction between their uses in Scripture.

However, one can quickly see how important the healing of our soul is for the higher function of our entire being. This holds great import when I introduce you to the *30 Days in His Glory Meditations and Devotional* in the following chapters.

But in the following chapter, we're going to shift our attention back to where it all began—in Genesis, when man was created out of the dust of the earth.

8

OUT OF THE DUST

*For you formed my inward parts; you knitted
me together in my mother's womb. I praise
you, for I am fearfully and wonderfully made*
(Psalm 139:13-14 ESV).

IF WE ARE TO CARE FOR OUR SOUL AND FULFILL THE
duty that God has assigned to each and every one of us,
we must understand our divine architecture or the fabric of the soul. This fabric can be fragile. After all, birth is
the beginning of the journey called life, and it brings both
good and bad, and God is our destination. Mortal life is a
process of unfolding or a sacred pilgrimage lived out from

stage to stage, and from birth to death, and to life everlasting. It is *the* adventure.

In following my previous comments, I turn our attention to the book of Genesis: *"And the Lord God formed a man of the dust of the ground, and breathed into his nostrils the breath of life; and man became a living **soul**"* (Genesis 2:7 KJV).

At that point, Adam became a composite creation, one comprised of a tri-unity of body, soul, and spirit. Hebraically, he is considered a unit of two—body and soul. But walk with me for a few moments and allow me to unpack this further.

Let's say the spirit is the command center, the soul is the brain center, and the body is the physical out-working of the spirit and soul. In other words, the soul is either driven by the Spirit of God or the carnal nature of a man. The spirit moves upon the soul and mobilizes the body. The body responds to the soul—and the soul responds to the spirit. If the body is in danger the soul will respond to fear and can activate—fight or flight! On the other hand, the spirit can cause the body to follow in a new command—faith. Smith Wigglesworth said, "Fear is to look; faith is to jump."

Let me coax you forward a bit more.

Within each of us is a divinely wired mechanization that takes place every moment of every day of our entire lives, through whatever situation we find ourselves. It's happening right now in our time together. How you're processing my story, for instance. But it's everywhere. It is either for God or for self. And here of course is the rub.

The soul by its inherent fallen nature wants to go rogue; it always wants to take over without the Spirit of God. This is fundamentally rooted in the Adamic fall. Paul's letter to the Romans says, *"For what I want to do I do not do, but what I hate I do. ...For I know that good itself does not dwell in me"* (Romans 7:15,18). *He is speaking about the inherent rogue nature that is our sinful nature.* "For I have the desire to do what is good, but I cannot carry it out" (Romans 7:18).

What we have seen is that the spirit can respond to the soul as the soul can respond to the spirit. Paul's words reveal that the spirit of God through faith has infused his entire being with a new spirit man, and this spirit man has given his soul a new desire.

Wonderful. Supernatural. But now his body must follow in good. Yet he struggles. The mind needs to be stronger. The body needs to be weaker. In this way the spirit can take greater dominion over the body and soul.

Galatians 5:17 states, *"For the flesh desires what is contrary to the Spirit, and the Spirit what is contrary to the flesh. They are in conflict with each other, so that you are not to do whatever you want."* Again, this is not a devil issue but a soul issue. The soul must be in continual subjection to the spirit. This is why the psalmist addresses his soul numerous times: "Why, O my soul, are you troubled?"

Back to Galatians. What is the flesh after all?

A partnership between the body and the soul. But true kingdom partnership takes place between the spirit and the soul. The body simply follows as the soul follows the spirit, so we fulfill the duty that God has assigned to us.

I know what you're thinking: "Thank you, now I'm really confused!"

I lean back against my chair to rest a bit as I am writing this. I'm tired. Because at times my heart is caught in my throat between excitement and the need to share with you all of my new discoveries.

We are in unconventional waters here, aren't we?

If you are pondering my words, you have joined my adventure. Hopefully, you have become visibly introspective, and you are feeling that deep thread, which we all have, being pulled.

Well, let's begin to get to the meat of it!

Let's discover the psalmist's soul, because God introduced me to him within the first three days of my return.

9

THE PSALMIST'S SOUL

*Why, my soul, are you downcast? Why so
disturbed within me? Put your hope in God,
for I will yet praise him, my Savior and my
God* (Psalm 42:11).

I REMEMBER THE MORNING. IT WAS THE FIRST DAY FOL-
lowing my return and the Lord said, "You will be in only
two books, Psalms and Ezekiel." He said: *"You will eat
from these two books alone for eight months."* And I did!
Psalms and Ezekiel. Nothing else passed through my heart
and mind for that entire period. Ezekiel would serve as a
source of new understanding for our call to the Jewish

people, but Psalms would begin a deep internal upheaval of all that I have ever known.

I discovered the psalmist to be highly intuitive when it came to his soul. He saw a man's soul poverty stricken, dark, and grey. The psalmist spoke directly to his soul. Then, in the midst of the 66 books of the Bible, I discovered the "Handbook of the Soul."

Yes! It's Psalms!

It contains 61 Psalms and 225 verses that teach us about giving God glory and magnifying Him. Fifty percent of the book of Psalms focuses upon the magnification and enlargement of God. But it speaks about the soul more than any other book. It's the handbook on how to magnify and enlarge God in your life as well as understanding the relationship between our soul and spirit.

We learn the purpose of the soul and how to treat and protect it. This lone part of the Bible would serve as my instruction for not 30 days but over one year. In the first three days of my return, it would give birth to a new heavenly daily regimen—30 Days in His Glory—which will be offered to you at the end of the book.

The psalmist taught me about my relationship to my soul. The soul can be estranged from the womb (58:3). It waits and thirsts for God (62:1-2; 63:1-2). The soul needs to cling to God (63:8), and the psalmist tells his soul what God has done (66:16).

We learn that God draws near to the soul and gladdens the soul (69:18). Then he commands his soul to bless the Lord (103:1-5). The soul waits for the Lord, and your soul is strengthened by Him. The soul was created to worship the Lord in the splendor of His majesty.

In Proverbs 20:27 it says, *"The spirit* [soul] *of man is the candle of the Lord"* (KJV). If we successfully discipline and harness the soul, the candle burns brighter. Keep the soul taut, the flame enlarges. In other words, whenever you choose to make known the will of God, the soul there goeth, my friend, and the candle burns brighter.

You see, I want to awaken something in you as God awakened in me. No! I need to awaken something more in you. I want you to have what I received! Can you see that we have entered into a higher place now in our journey? This topic is vital.

DROWNING OUR SOUL

Friend, our souls can undergo many wounds in life that build up like layers that can form a thick callus. As I noted earlier, the soul is like a fragile cloth. Sometimes it seems as though we're doomed to sink in the Red Sea of failure from the seasons of tearing and pulling. But when the waters are just about to go over our heads, we make one last effort to find our safe haven again, and we have endured another season of trial, right?

I have concluded that there is a simple and declarative taking of our joy in life that happens to many, and there is an entire topic of teaching which we have had no exposure to—the healing of our souls. After all, we are on this road of life for 70 or 80 years or more, and we can hit many bumps along the way.

Our soul can be like an old car, dented and beat up. Our emotions can end up like a well—capped off. Our soul can feel as though it is drowning in life's difficulties and disappointments. So it must be cleansed, rebooted, and unstopped.

But I found the secret that has been hiding under our noses. Truly!

The heavenly and scriptural teachings, the gift that awaits you at the end of this book, are not based upon psychology or therapy, but solely on the work of the Holy Spirit and the Word of God, both working in harmony with the glory of His presence.

GIFT OF CONSCIOUSNESS

Certainly, consciousness of sin and assurance of grace through our Messiah are two great truths and arsenals of healing. It's preventative for sure. But I am not speaking about the eternal destiny of our soul that is fixed in the blood of Yeshua either.

If you haven't noticed, this conversation is about living victoriously on a higher plane, both spiritually and physically. A healthy soul leads to a healthy body. *"Do not be wise in your own eyes; fear the Lord and shun evil. This will bring health to your body and nourishment to your bones"* (Proverbs 3:7-8).

To understand the soul, we find ourselves in a deep mining exercise where we must begin to think of how we were created to operate and live with an abiding presence in our life. Understanding death in the next chapter helps us discover more about our soul.

10

What I Learned About Life and Death

WHAT I AM ABOUT TO SHARE WITH YOU FROM MY LIFE and death, is again unconventional. Death. Life. Afterlife. I want to bring this topic out of the shadows.

Before my experience, I always saw our lives as part of a greater spiritual reality that transcended birth, death, time, and space. For reasons that I have not fully come to understand, my Lord's mercy restored my life. As God saved me that day, I believe He did this to allow me to tell others about it for the remainder of my earthly days.

You see, I found death to be as beautiful as birth. A difficult concept to grasp, I know. After all, it is hard for us when those who have once brought us joy then pass on, leaving only their memory to fill the dark emptiness that their death can bring. As I have said earlier, I saw Bonnie distraught and grieving as I was in the spiritual realm.

I could see us now huddled together at this point.

"How is it possible that death is as beautiful as birth?" you are asking yourself, right?

But I can come up with no better way of saying it, and even then, I'm not sure that I would do it justice.

DEATH AND BIRTH

Death. Birth. Both are generally preceded by pain, then followed by joy, particularly when a newborn child is placed for the first time on a mother's chest. Death—the body's electrical impulse shuts off like a switch, and all things material, body, tissue, muscle, tendon, and bone, begin to return to earthen clay. Although it is the immediate cessation of your physical life, something glorious and wonderful occurs when the spirit enters another glorious dimension.

Whatever the circumstances that cause it, the second the body is ready to give up the spirit, something congruent with our original design takes place.

You see, the morning my spirit checked out of my body, the crossing over was met with an instant lightning bolt of joy, peace, and tranquility. It felt wonderful and freeing, as if I was leaving a hotel room to enter through another door. In one fluid motion, my spirit naturally and harmoniously stepped out of the confines of my physical frame.

This is what happens.

Friend, having this conversation is important.

Wouldn't you like to know the joy and tranquility that your loved one felt?

Surely!

The idea of knowing where your spirit will go while you have the chance to decide is like being hit by a meteor of a new awareness and urgency. Knowing the joy that a loved one experienced when they died becomes a source of joy. It's not only the glory of Heaven that awaits them, but the glorious journey once they cross over. Heaven is glorious, and so is the process in crossing over.

If you are reading this and you don't know where your spirit will go upon death, pray now! Pause to ask the Lord to come into your life through a simple prayer provided at the end of this chapter. If you need to turn to that page now, do so. Then come back so we can learn how to walk through doors together.

WALKING THROUGH DOORS

When considering life as we are together, isn't it true that we walk through doors throughout days and weeks that build up to years? Maybe 70, 80, or 90 years as the Lord gives. We simply arise, walk, and leave the room as we always have for a thousand times never thinking anything about it. Life seems to script our lives to a daily routine. Days, months, and years race by with no thought of eternity.

You may have started your life with a clear identity, with a very defined picture of who you wanted to be and how you saw yourself getting there.

Perhaps over the years the waves of adversity and disappointment began eating away at your goals and ambitions until your life reached a crisis stage.

Perhaps your situation has become so obtrusive that you finally recognize the years of erosion and your hopes have all but dwindled.

To every individual I meet, I now say, "Your soul will enter the same miraculous dimension one day."

I explain my story to person after person. As certain as the sun rises and as the sun sets, life can end abruptly. It's over, that's it!

No more chances to change.

No more personal theories of the afterlife.

No more opportunities to decide.

In that moment you will either rise to the glories of Heaven, or what I saw, and I shudder to even say it, crash land in hell. Terrible. I tremble at the latter.

What will it be like for you?

Dare I ask where you are in this life, friend?

And what things consume your days?

Money. Yourself. Fruitless activities. Endless shopping. Busyness. Building. Planning. Are you one of the prestigious multi-billionaires on your way to being a trillionaire?

Surely, I am concerned for one's soul in these moments. I think of what I might say to the many millionaires or billionaires today who have it all. Some who might think that their extraordinary successes have handed them the power to control the winds, the rain, the moon, and the stars. That time starts and stops within the universe of their control. Well, only God holds those powers in His hands!

I'm actually here to tell you that you can have it all!

That's right, my friend!

You can enjoy the vast fortunes of your labor here, while in eternity enjoy the vast majesty of Heaven. It's not a sin to be rich! It's a tragedy to go to hell and have decay and sorrow for all eternity as a result of your earthly pursuits.

You see, God made life and death, and he made the wealthy and the poor. God does not despair in saving millionaires, billionaires, or future trillionaires. God is the one who gave you the ability to amass your wealth. His Son died for you, and He wants you home with your heavenly Father when your time is up.

But it will take some forethought on your part. Perhaps a moment of reflection to consider God's gift of eternal life is appropriate. Perhaps it is no coincidence that we are having this conversation.

A JUDGMENT TO COME

You see, there is point that needs to be stressed here. I am only too aware of the judgment that awaits every soul, whether they are rich or poor. You can feel my strong tilt toward this topic. It's part of me now as never before. I haven't known such strong feelings in a very long time. These are weighty moments. It's like a heavy pendulum that may or may not swing the right way. I am referring to your heart!

So what are people waiting for?

What are you waiting for?

Something of an eternal nature swoops down on my soul right now. It's an indescribable joy.

Why, you might ask?

Well, let me offer you these queries:

What is a joy so unexplainable, so absorbing, and so complete that words are insufficient to describe it?

What is a joy so unexplainable that you know that your soul is inseparable from your heavenly Father, a joy so penetrating that no matter how death comes it holds no terror, and you cannot be moved from an unexplainable sense of security?

If you don't know that kind of joy that I speak of, *you need to!*

But again, are you ready?

PRAYER FOR TRANSFORMATION

If you want that peace, tranquility, and joy you can pray a simple prayer as I did many decades ago:

> *Lord, forgive me of my sins and come into my life as my Lord, Savior, and Messiah. Thank You for sending Yeshua, Jesus, as the Lamb of God for me. I ask You to come into my life and make me a child of God.*

11

THE SECRET INGREDIENT: TRANSFORMATIONAL PRAYER

MISINFORMATION AND PRAYER CULTURE

At last! There is now another story that I have been anxious to begin with you. It will prepare you to receive that gift that I noted in the beginning of the book. Remember, the one that has been hiding right under our noses. I referred to it as a miracle ingredient, and that ingredient is *transformational prayer.*

Here I am, sitting in my chair contemplating what I am about to share with you. I know that it is critical as well as life changing. At times I can feel frozen in time only considering how to confront our prayer culture with you, because it critical to the quality of our lives as believers and the key to greater power in the last days.

But here we go!

In the following pages, I will show you what this is and how you can create transformational space in your prayer life that will release a transforming power into your daily life. First, I must show you how to be free of a spirit of need. Once this is done, transformational prayer will blow the lid off the top of your life, and your instinctive prayer patterns will find a new expression. I call it living under a sky and no longer under a ceiling.

You see, we have been programed wrongly in the area of prayer and our current default mode of prayer, which is limiting. But no longer.

TRANSFORMATIONAL PRAYER

You are now about to *spot* something. A prayer life that is not transactional in form, which is our default, but one that is glory building, God enlarging, and earth defying. It can sound like an infomercial promising a magic tonic for all of our ills. But all of what I have just stated regarding this new prayer form is 100 percent true and is available to you. Furthermore, it is 100 percent biblical.

For all the years of my faith, over 45 years now, my soul was smothered by certain misinformation in our training and culture in the area of prayer. Until one day in September of 2019, the Spirit of God began to introduce me to a more heavenly prayer model.

It happened within three days of my return from the third heaven, when I would be placed in a new spiritual regimen that would introduce me to a new operating system. It's what I have been setting the stage for, so you can have it.

Of course, my journey into the heavenlies is not transferable, and perhaps difficult to relate to. One must go through an after-death or out-of-body experience to comprehend it. But the residue of Heaven that I returned with is a new operating system, or I like to say *Heaven's operating system.*

You see, three days after my return, I had no desire to remain on earth and live in the old system. We can look up to the towering hillside of tradition, but I became tired of a monotonous prayer life that characterizes most of church culture.

Then I began to feel a surge of something, and I instantly recognized a new system of spiritual living. Pure and overwhelmingly real, I began to consider the value of my soul and submerge it under the glory and magnification of God. It would last not three days or even three months; it's continuing on for 18 months now and counting!

This heavenly gift is yours, and it is the joyful climax of this book. I call it *30 Days in His Glory Meditations and Devotional.*

My purpose is nothing short of wanting to launch you into this new operating system. The Lord showed me that Heaven's atmosphere is possible to experience in a greater reality once we get out from under the weight of a transactional prayer life. I know you're wondering what it is. Hold on, my friend, we are getting closer.

You might also be wondering if this system works, and is it sustainable?

Well, I can't wait to get before the Lord for prayer every morning now since September of 2019. I still feel like I can see for miles. I look up in a room and feel like a sky is overhead and no longer a ceiling. I pray to the Lord and leave my needs with my heavenly Father. I trust Him. I do not need to keep reminding Him of my needs by praying for the same thing again and again.

Let's be forthright.

A wiser course was well expressed in the meaning of Yeshua's words in Matthew 11:28-30:

> Come to me, all you who are weary and **burdened**, and I will give you **rest**. Take **my yoke upon** you and learn from me, for I am gentle and humble of heart, and you will find **rest** for your souls. **For my yoke is easy, and my burden is light.**

The word *rest* means tranquility for your soul, *peace*, and *shalom!* It's like a temporary respite that soldiers are given. This tranquility was promised by the Lord for our entire temporal life. In Hebrew, Shalom also means, He who destroys the authority that establishes chaos. The question is, "How do we maintain and live in it?"

LINES OF CONFLICT

To understand this secret ingredient, there are some major lines of conflict to consider that run through our society and, most importantly, the community of faith. Up until now we have had no control over them.

I realized upon my return that something was missing along the way throughout my own prayer life. My reason, of course, was a good one—I sensed a new system upon my return, and I immediately recognized the limitations of the former. Heaven established a new context and construct for living, so I asked, "Why didn't I discover this 45 years ago?"

The first line of conflict is perhaps the fact that few people have crossed over and returned to talk about the nature of our topic, *transformational prayer*. Certainly, the only reason this writing is taking place is because of my time in Heaven, and the 90 days of glory that I experienced following my brief immortality.

Second, any new or revamped version of some religious thought always catches one by surprise, as does revival, renewal, and spiritual outpouring. It challenges religious authority and tradition itself, because it's in the DNA of revivals.

Third, and perhaps the most important, our prayers are mainly optimized around need. Yes, earth is a need-based environment. So for a good reason our prayers are need-based. But if we consign the days of our life to a wearisome, daily, need-based prayer life that is transactional in nature, we can never experience a daily heavenly atmosphere. This was not the intention of our heavenly Father.

He wanted us to have peace and shalom, and not be weighed down with the same requests day in and day out, living with the weight of our burdens. Remember His promise, "For my yoke is easy, and my burden is *light*."

Last, traditional prayer models promote importunity, perseverance, fervency, intensity, and not letting go until the answer comes. Rightfully. Jacob wrestled with the angel and didn't let go; Moses pleaded with God over and over to forgive the sins of the Israelites when they turned to false idols; Elijah told his servant to go back seven times to look for the cloud as he labored in prayer.

There are times for importunity.

At the same time, this should not be *the* way of life if we want to break a needy spirit in our prayer life. We must move from the transactional to the transformational. So, I want to *stop* you long enough, so you can *spot* something, and then *swap* for a new system.

Let me also say, that this new prayer model is a special ingredient that you will introduce into your current prayer life. What will change is the right balance, once we challenge convention in the next chapter.

12

CHALLENGING CONVENTION

HEAVEN WILL ALWAYS CHALLENGE CONVENTION, AND also, man is bedazzled by the practical world of convention. It feeds his flesh and intellect. It also smothers a substantive spiritual existence. Worse, it hinders the substance of faith. You know, *"the substance of things hoped for, the evidence of things not seen"* (Hebrews 11:1 NKJV).

Faith is anything but conventional. Smith Wigglesworth said, "Fear looks, faith jumps." I have a picture of clipping the flight feathers from a bird when I think of convention and religion.

Conventional feels comfortable—chocolate or vanilla, black or white, that's it. I have always been prompted to seek more because there is more, much more. You likely feel the same. After all, you have joined me in the telling of my adventure.

Convention, you see, is our enemy. Convention makes it difficult to detach and *stop* long enough so you can *spot* a weakness. COVID-19 was a forced *stop* for the world, and the opportunity to learn detachment. Many opportunities came to *spot* weaknesses. Only then are you ready to *swap* for something better.

So yes, convention is the enemy of grand faith. You know what faith is. Call things that are not as though they are. When our desperation spontaneously springs forth with a new spiritual hunger, it can become like a gusher from the ground that begins to water a new prayer movement for change.

What happens then?

We *stop*, then *spot* our own desperate spiritual state, to get ready to *swap* for a revival in our lives. This was the formula for my own personal revival decades ago. So, yes! Yes! The entire spiritual dimension is unconventional.

Surely, from the crossing over of my spirit following cardiac arrest, to the rising into the third heaven, then visiting the second heaven, only to have an angel minister to my soul, it's all unconventional.

The entire book of Acts is unconventional, as are the gifts of the spirit in 1 Corinthians 12. What of the apostle Paul who was taken into the third heaven; John on the island of Patmos ascended to Heaven to receive a vision of the seven churches. Miracles of all proportions are unconventional.

Even in the natural this battle ensues. Thomas Edison's eyes hurt him every time he tried to read by the light of an oil lamp. He asked himself, "Why can't I discover something to take the place of the oil lamp?" Conventional thought cited him as crazy. He had faith in his dream by inventing the electric light bulb. He challenged conventional thinking and dared to ask, "Is there a better way?"

Many hundreds of years ago the wise men of Israel spoke of a brotherhood of man where love would rule the world. Today, we call those men prophets. Others call them dreamers. As yet their dream has not come true, but its power is so great that it will become real in the coming kingdom to earth. And so it is with every dreamer who boldly stood against convention.

Friend, I urge you to become a dreamer. Imagine a new prayer life that will transform you. As I show you what happened to me, I am going to suggest a set of actions that will open the sky over your life so you are no longer living under a ceiling.

To understand the *transformational* realm, which is the polar opposite of conventional, is to reframe your prayer life in a transformational space. This prayer life is never static, but it is always moving your spirit and heart toward God. It is wholly biblical. It's effortlessly performed. It is immediately rewarding.

I know you are saying, "What is it already?"

But you see, somewhere back in our history it was lost. A mystery! A secret waiting to be discovered. And as I have stated repeatedly, it's been hiding right under our noses.

BRINGING BALANCE

Giving time for my previous words to be absorbed, I am carefully taking you closer step by step.

First, prayer has always been the linchpin to blessing and allows the movement of God. The psalmist states, *"Hear my voice, O God, in my complaint; preserve my life"* (Psalm 64:1 ESV). Then, *"You who answer prayer, to you all people will come"* (Psalm 65:2). Prayer is the pathway and enterprise of individual growth and spiritual advancement. Paul says to pray unceasingly. I have not forgotten his words in his first letter to the Thessalonians 5:16-18.

The word *pray* is mentioned close to 500 times in the scriptures, and *prayer* is mentioned close to 100 times. Pray. This is clearly the message. Make it a business of prayer, and be serious and earnest in doing so. Whatever you pray, pray according to God's promises, and it shall be given to you if God sees fit to give it! And what more would you have?

So yes, always pray!

The culture of the body from which our good Father came and gave us His Son has adapted the custom to ask and receive, believe and claim, and to go repeatedly to the Father, which is indeed good medicine, right? But prayer is not to be used only when one is in deep trouble either. We're supposed to pray to God in our joys and in our successes.

There is a rabbinic saying that goes: "Honor thy physician when thou hast no need for him." This means that we must pray not only when we are in pain or want (transactional), but also when we are not in need (transformational). *"Come unto the Lord in rejoicing,"* says the psalmist.

So I am not saying to stop praying!

Heavens, no!

At the same time, a constant need-based prayer life pulls down upon our soul and acts like weights connected to the edges of a fabric. It fosters an insufficiency mindset, which we speak more about later, and can leave one frustrated and disappointed with God.

For this reason, I see spiritual poverty in a prayer life without a robust exaltation space.

You see, in my years of experience in serving the Lord, I have seen the altars filled with the same people with the same needs.

Why? God is not a respecter of persons, nor has He changed. He is the same yesterday, today, and tomorrow.

One may consider my comments to be unfair since many problems in people's lives are no fault of their own. But the point is, problems are inherent on earth, and we will always have them. But how are we to rise above them? Isn't that the challenge that Yeshua wanted us to meet, to cast our burdens upon Him? He was actually asking us to change ownership of our burdens. The same understanding is in 1 Peter 5:7: *"Cast all your anxiety on him because he cares for you."*

MEETING THE CHALLENGE

In meeting the challenge, I was given help. I was given a gift. A prayer life defined by magnification and exaltation that no longer build on an old rutty framework of insufficiency. Today, my pray life is framed in a construct of complete sufficiency and the life abundant (John 10:10).

This prayer model will lead to smaller altars, and more service-minded people will come for prayer and greater anointing in their lives. In fact, it will put the counselors and phycologists in the church out of business. It will, in fact, mitigate the insufficiency mindsets that many struggle with. If we always come before God with our needs, we miss one of the finest aims of prayer, which you will discover as you read on.

Also, resist the gasp of disbelief, perhaps, at the suggestion to only pray the transformational way—exaltation and magnification as a matter of course. Here I will show you the proper balance with a heavenly formula. It will restore the right proportion of transformation and transaction.

13

ARE YOU TIRED
OF THE OLD YET?

IF WE ARE TO *STOP* AND *SWAP* FOR SOMETHING BETTER, we must be tired of an older operating system. Perhaps you have begun to *spot* the hint of what a transactional prayer life is. Here is my testimony.

In the *30 Days in His Glory Devotional and Meditation* I took a vacation from my prayer needs. I have actually been on a prayer-needs vacation since September 2019 because I love the freedom. I pray throughout the day, as Paul says to pray unceasingly, but my appointment with God in the morning is filled with exaltation and magnification. My days have been changed to absorbing my Father's beauty, glory, and His creative fingerprint everywhere. My mind is permanently fixed on the things above.

Over that period, I have seen my prayers answered. I pray and I leave them with my Father because I trust Him—*I have transferred ownership, you see!*

Throughout my glory devotional, I have been in a select portion of what I call "Glory Psalms," discovered by the direction of the Lord, and I have remained in them since my return from heaven. Let me tell you, an insufficiency mindset has been replaced with one of sufficiency, and all of this came about because I was tired of an old operating system, or a prayer culture that lacked transformative elements.

Now, let's get to the root of it.

The part I do not like about our current prayer culture is that it is driven by transactional mindsets that are rooted in an insufficiency mindset. Which, by the way, you've probably been thinking about a lot now. That is good, because it will help you make the *switch*.

When engaged in transformational prayer, your focus is upon *His* glory! The obvious benefits enables us to move into a more service mindset. Insufficiency no longer crowds our mind with needs, which gives freedom to our soul. This allows more room in our hearts to serve God and others as our soul is less taxed by the earthly.

It should also be noted that money is not the key to a sufficiency mindset. Many wealthy people never have enough money and are always counting what they have; it's called a spirit of poverty or shortage. A billionaire can have a spirit of shortage, while a poor person can have spirit of abundance.

When Paul asked the Lord to remove a thorn from his side, something that had become an annoyance in his life and likely tormented him at times, God said *no!* "My grace will be sufficient." In that moment he moved from insufficiency to sufficiency, he changed the ownership, and it was the end of the matter as far as we can see. You see, as long as we remain in insufficiency mindsets, prayers and thoughts remain on needs, and our service to God is hampered.

What is the answer?

We must change the relationship of ownership—give our burdens and cares to the *One* who owns them. I gave Him my thorns because He took them on His back for me. Then my insufficiency became my sufficiency. When my eyes were opened to this, I saw an entire faith community immersed in a need-based transactional prayer culture.

Consider—most all relationships, with the exception of marriage, are transactional. Working relationships, ministry relationships, platonic, and yes, perhaps even romantic can all bear this mark. Often, we carefully calculate what we can ask in return.

To a certain degree, sacrifice is no longer in vogue as well. The forgotten art of submission means the loss of too much of our self. People find it more difficult today to detach themselves from themselves because they are not living in a sufficiency mindset.

It all takes its toll on relationships.

Intimacy, on the other hand, is about sacrifice and fulfillment, which comes from a service mindset. This is what the life of Yeshua is all about. He sacrificed and served. But our culture is acutely counter.

In today's times, social media epitomizes selfishness in a grand way. People maintain their secret rooms. On Facebook, they show only what they want to show and embellish on the positive, always sequestering the negative. Often, the dearest and closest are shielded from what and who they really are. We can also become experts in keeping things from our own consciousness.

In our secret lab, we formulate our plans, keep score, count, and plan for our own needs, but our math is never straightforward, right? It's always a little biased toward our end. This danger, or secret cunning, poisons the design of real intimacy, and indeed deeper levels of transformation.

How can we share life if we are individuals operating as secret enemies, or spies who are trading openly under the guise of sacrifice and friendship? We have maxims like: What's in it for me? I'll scratch your back if you scratch mine, and *quid pro quo*. We don't even know we're doing it until we burst out with a "You owe me!"

Hence, how much of our prayers are transactional versus transformational? Let me also say, individuals are not at fault; it lies with our corporate prayer culture and perhaps the world we live in today.

OUR PRAYER CULTURE

Let's get real! Prayers are generally about us—help me, give us, do a miracle, send Your Holy Spirit, give us understanding, heal Mary Jones, heal me or us or him, please, thank You, etc. These prayers are all about asking God to do something or give something or function in some way that will benefit us or others. Personal needs dominate our prayers.

Today it's COVID-19. Several years back it was the real estate collapse, and decades ago, it was the Great Recession. The personal needs in our daily, weekly, and monthly lives will always be with us. Children, grandchildren, the needs of the church, society, government, and our ministries—the list goes on and on. Our answered prayers today are replaced with new ones tomorrow. In most cases, the list just grows.

In my life as a believer, I cannot remember when I was without multiple prayer needs.

Will we ever be without needs? Never!

We can close our eyes tightly and pretend it's not there, but when you open them, the majority of our prayer life is consumed with trying to move the hand of God for answers. There may be exceptions, of course, as with anything, but in the real world, a shift needs to take place, given the last-days trials that are fast upon us. God is greater and has a better system for us all, and it's called praying Heaven's way!

14

Praying Heaven's Way

Transformational Prayer

Building upon the former chapter, we know that we cannot love one another in the truest sense of the word without sharing all that we are. It's called transparency and sacrifice.

To be sure, the limits of our ability to connect with others—i.e., lack of transparency and intimacy—do carry into our relationship with the Lord. Passages like, *"Carry each other's burdens, and in this way you will fulfill the law of Christ"* or, *"No one should seek their own good, but the good of others"* (Galatians 6:2; 1 Corinthians 10:24).

Yeshua taught us that love is about sacrificing yourself for a greater good. It sounds like a paradox, but it is the true makeup of a healthy relationship and the embodiment of our Lord. In fact, it is the substance of the kingdom on earth.

But let's take the next step into praying Heaven's way.

I noted previously, a prayer life dominated by need and absent of exaltation fosters a needy spirit or an insufficiency mindset. This can leave one frustrated, worried, and emotionally drained.

A life in ministry has demonstrated this again and again. I have witnessed far too many times when people have their burdens return like a boomerang, which causes them to lose peace, causing unrest again in their soul. This has always pained my heart and caused me to be circumspect about the fragility of people's pain. But this is all a good indicator of the limits of a transactional prayer life.

How do we detach from our needs?

How do we get liberation from our needs?

How do we change the ownership of these burdens?

My own transformational-based prayer was the liberator of my soul. Upon my return, and within the first three days, I set out every morning in a transformational prayer governed by the majesty and grandeur of God. My soul was then pulled upward, as the psalmist commanded his soul to worship the Lord, because God is the lifter of our heads and our souls.

Worry over the COVID-19 lifted. No longer did my personal prayer needs govern my earliest morning time with the Lord. I was starving my soul you see, of the natural order, and drowning it in exaltation of God. Then, something extraordinary began to occur. All of a sudden I was praying Heaven's way. I found what Paul wrote to the Colossians, and effortlessly it became the normal course of my days. Heaven began to seat itself in my soul through and through.

> *Since, then, you have been raised with Christ, set your hearts on things above, where Christ is, seated at the right hand of God. Set your minds on things above, not on earthly things* (Colossians 3:1-2).

It's important to make this critical distinction. Transformational prayer sets your mind above earthly things. You don't strive for it; it happens.

Also these words in Philippians 4:6-7:

> *Be anxious for nothing, but in everything by prayer and supplication, with thanksgiving, let your requests be made known to God; and the peace of God, which surpasses all understanding, will guard your hearts and minds through Christ Jesus* (NKJV).

Notice the promise of a peace that surpasses all understanding. This peace is not supposed to be temporary.

You will find that in this new system, when your thought life becomes conscious of your heavenly Father's greatness and grandeur every day, you find there is no room for insufficiency. This has continued since September 2019, because this new operating system is wholly biblical, God honoring, earth defying, and heavenly focused.

PRAYER IN HEAVEN: I WANT IT!

What I discovered in Heaven was that there were no prayer needs as we are accustomed to here on earth, only exaltation and magnification of the Father. "Of course," you say. Everyone is redeemed. Even though there is intercession for the earthly saints going on daily (Revelation 5:8; 6:9-11). But I take you back to these words, *"Since, then, you have been raised with Christ, set your hearts on things above, where Christ is, seated at the right hand of God. Set your minds on things above, not on earthly things."*

What are the things above? Heaven! Glory! I was so moved by this transformational environment that upon my return I was prompted to mimic Heaven's atmosphere with my earthly prayer life, so I immediately asked the Lord to show me the way.

When I began, my silence before the Lord was no longer tainted by desires and wants (sufficiency), knowing that they would only detract me from the living, present glory that was now descending. Even vague impressions from the past would try and break through. Often shadowy images of my future would attempt to lay siege to my silence.

The Lord told me to let my silence not be filled with thoughts or fleeting ideas and concepts. Rather, to let my silence be confined by time and space open to infinity—yes, infinity! We can live under an infinite sky whereby each day you become mindful of His handprint everywhere. I call this an adventure!

Immediately, I said goodbye to prayers that had *I, me, us, we,* and *mine*. The majority of my time in prayer was focused upon Him, You Lord, Master, King, and Creator.

Notice the difference?

Know also that I still petitioned the Lord with my needs, but differently. My petitions began to emerge throughout the day, praying more as Paul said to pray unceasingly. But always, my first early morning hours were upon Him and Him alone.

In other words, my conventional prayers of petition were replaced with exaltations and magnifications of our Lord in all His glory. The meditations of the psalmist penetrated my soul and brought my soul back into alignment with Heaven's atmosphere. It all began a circular motion, rather than linear, and I found myself increasingly detached from this earthly life.

Sounds wonderful, right?

Let me tell you the greatest benefit.

NO MORE WEIGHTINESS

The daily benefit is that your soul will be less weighed down with the needs in your life as an insufficiency mindset is broken. Which will make you will feel more tethered to your spiritual identity. Heavenly mindedness will seat itself in your day, and a lightness will be in your step again.

I noted earlier that the transformational prayer life is one that extols the greatness and the majesty of God. These personal addresses to God first come from select portions found in book of Psalms that are provided at the end of this book. These are for your daily sacred space to launch you into a new operating system.

When you *stop* the old so you can *spot* the new, you will *swap* for this new operating system, I assure you.

I must also be clear. I offer no set formula or program here. It must be accompanied with a desire and heart attitude and born out of your soul. All of this must come to us when we are tired of the old and thirsty for something new and restorative. God is waiting for you to exclaim, "Hineni—here I am, O Father."

WIRED FOR TRANSFORMATION

Lastly, it's important to realize that God's people are divinely wired to be transformational, which is circular in form. Everything God creates is circular. The planets, moon, sun, blood cells, a woman's egg, and a human embryo. When a raindrop falls to earth it disperses in a circular fashion, and so on (Proverbs 8:12). Prophecy, on the other hand, runs linearly, and our relationship is vertical, but life is circular, and we represent the highest divine order in His creation.

You see, only God is involved in circular creation. Other shapes like squares represent a partnership between God and man. But circular involves God alone.

Once we become a child of God, we are designed to live in sufficiency mindsets throughout the circular duration of our days in life. We call these seasons. We can also say that insufficiency is earthly and linear; sufficiency is heavenly and circular.

By way of illustration, on the rocks and reefs of the sea we find plant life so deeply rooted that they are almost impossible to remove. Yet the only changes occur by the natural ebb and flow of the current. How terrible for a child of God to be so rooted in the linear things and concerns of this life that the only variety that they see is due to natural ebb and flow of life itself. Day after day, their life is dictated by earthly events—a soul cleaving to the soil.

Is it not His voice calling us higher, to in fact uproot ourselves from the earthly rock and soil we are stuck in?

Friend, God promised so much more!

As we go from glory to glory in life, one precept upon another, from knowledge to deeper knowledge, circular again, we are being transformed into His image with intensifying glory (2 Corinthians 3:17-18), moving us into transformational living. Take Paul's critical teaching on the believer's armor in Ephesians 6; there is no protection in the back, because we are wired only to move forward. Hence, the believer's life should never be static!

When I discovered transformational prayer, I felt like I had discovered the holy grail of living! My life seemed to be moving again to new and higher glory levels. Circularly, I was moving again. And although this increasing glory life came by way of my brief journey to Heaven through my life-and-death experience, the Lord assured me that others can experience it without dying. Everyone can reboot their prayer life and orient their soul upward into a more heavenly atmosphere.

Too be sure, before my departure my life was rooted in our current transactional prayer culture like everyone. It's all we have ever known. This is important, because the most important aspect of our prayers is the degree to which we spend all of our time transacting with God for something. Imagine your children always coming home to transact with you about something, as opposed to spending time with you.

We obviously speak quite a bit about transactional versus transformational here, but it's time to define it more concisely.

Transactional prayer is seen in an action to receive, while transformational prayer is an action to give. That's why transformational prayer is proactive and not static.

It orients our soul upward toward Heaven and moves us away from the earthly linear plane, which hinders our ability to detach from it. In Psalm 3:3, it says that the Lord is the lifter of our heads. Transformational prayer accomplishes this.

The truth of a transformational prayer life is sharply highlighted when our prayers are no longer like barnacles on a ship slowing us down, and we have more time to exalt our God in Heaven, and our life flow takes us into a new appreciation of His handprint everywhere in a given day. Make no mistake, God's handprint is everywhere.

15

MY GIFT TO YOU

30 DAYS IN HIS GLORY

My dear reader, by now you must be traveling through your mind perhaps trying to find an off-ramp to rest and absorb everything. Try to draw a picture in your mind of a prayer life that is predominantly giving glory to God and exalting Him daily when needs are no longer hogging all your time.

Imagine having fresh new insight as you recognize a fresh touch from your heavenly Father on a regular basis. Imagine starving your soul for a period of time of the natural order in the midst of your needs. When those giants become grasshoppers, your mountains become hills easily traversed, and God becomes larger and the earth smaller.

I should also mention, it's not done strenuously, but rather easily and gracefully. It is also self- sustainable.

Let's be honest—we need tools for increasing transformation. Our Messiah, the Bible, and the presence of the Holy Spirit are of course the most important. At the same time, God's people have a powerful weapon called prayer. Through the right kind of prayer, one can live upon a more elevated place and breathe what I call the "atmosphere of Heaven."

We have also entered a point in this work that brings us closer to the purpose of this writing. I've gotten you home, if you will, and the end is in sight. I'm anxious and a bit nervous, I will say! I hope when I'm finished, I sense relief and satisfaction from my Father that this recounting has been completed, and its message received—particularly the gift.

As I received an important teaching and discovery from the Lord through the book of Psalms, God wants everyone to discover it. It's too inspiring to miss it, so I want you to zoom into what the Spirit has directed me now. When you get it, you too will realize it's been hiding right under our noses.

Now, enough about me and my life-and-death experience. God wants you to capture something uniquely lovely within your soul.

So what's the plan?

Our Father did not despair in teaching us everything we need. He gave us 66 books to learn from, but one in particular flows abundantly in this topic—the book of Psalms. Over 60 psalms and well over two hundred verses are focused solely upon His glory, majesty, and all that He created.

Through these meditations, the Father shows us how the top comes off to free us, and opens the door into this transformational realm. When followed in the prescribed manner, these glory psalms become your personal prayers and keys to rebooting your system.

What system, you ask?

A system that will generate more heavenly mindedness and break off your burdens while setting your mind on things above rather than on earthly things. You will experience, in *30 Days in His Glory Meditations and Devotional*, a new freedom that will launch you into a transformational prayer life, or what I call a new operating system. I want you to imagine the effect upon your soul when you are set free from need, in the midst of need.

That's called a miracle!

It has been called the power of God.

Some call it the glory of God and the powerful grace of God, mainly because, supernaturally, complaining and worrying flee.

In other words, being set free of fear and worry in the midst of sickness is a miracle in itself. Believing for a financial breakthrough while one is homeless is miraculous. Believing is letting go and leaving your burdens with the Lord. That is the glory and power of God. But you must make a choice!

MAKING THE CHOICE

Much like any other physical cleansing system, our fast, a specific regimen, is followed in the 30 Days in His Glory. It is 100 percent God-centered, biblical, and glory-based. You should also know that you are about to face that choice I spoke of earlier in the book—whether this will be experiential or transformational. We're at this point because you are about to receive the gift that I received.

I predict that after the first three days you will increasingly appreciate the beauty of His creative work everywhere you go. God will push His way through your conventional thoughts and encourage you to follow upward in your thoughts. You will begin living more under the shimmer of His glory and experience what I receive each day through drops of heavenly grace in your daily life. In other words, *your perspective will change!*

But I give you a warning!

You'll find it's difficult to *only* exalt the Lord. This will be your greatest challenge. Go ahead and experiment. Try starving the soul of the natural order in order to give the Lord only glory in your prayer time with no petition, praise, thanksgiving, or intercession. You will discover if those earthly concerns control you. Try it for a day, two, and then for seven. You will see how difficult it really is. You need to be re-reprogramed, I assure you.

Yet the freedom that comes when you've broken free from convention releases a newly found mobility within your soul that you have never experienced before. You will follow in the words of the psalmist in 96:7-8, *"Ascribe to the Lord glory and strength. Ascribe to the Lord the glory due his name."*

Should you raise a hand to the Lord to accept this mission, a touch of Heaven will come surprisingly to you. I call it a kiss from our Creator. Might it be that we drown in the river of His delight after all, in such times that we need it the most?

16

Casting Your Burdens upon Him

Come to me, all you who are weary and burdened, and I will give you rest. Take my yoke upon you and learn from me, for I am gentle and humble in heart, and you will find rest for your souls. For my yoke is easy and my burden is light (Matthew 11:28-30).

Taking a Vacation

There are only two specific requirements for the *30 Days in His Glory Meditations and Devotional*—spend 30 days in complete adoration and magnification of God, and nothing else. I want you to take a 30-day vacation from your burdens.

Sounds unconventional, right?

Absolutely.

No petitions.

No thanksgiving or praise.

Only glory and magnification of our Creator.

Remember, it's only for one month out of an entire year that you will leave your burdens with your Father. But you may like it so much that you will likely leave them with your Father as I did.

In preparation to receive the gift that I have been promising—we are going to categorize our prayers by degrees, which is also unconventional, I know.

First-degree prayers are like S.O.S. prayers:

"Lord, we needed an answer yesterday!"

"We need healing today."

"We are losing our home, please help us, Lord."

"We need a financial breakthrough."

Considered first-degree prayers would be an accident, a tragedy, or something dire that has occurred. Obviously, things that are essential and urgent need immediate attention. Most others we consider second- and third-degree prayer needs. Prayers that we carry with us for a season, or perhaps even over the course of our lives. In fact, they occupy most of our prayers. Certainly, you can let go of these for 30 days, right? I assure you, they will be right there where you left them when you return from your vacation.

MAKING STRUCTURAL ADJUSTMENT

Taking a more critical view, we are going to adjust the formula. As a believer for over 45 years, serving in ministry for over three decades, I have observed that 75 percent of one's prayer life is spent on trying to move the hand of God and looking for answers. I would say that only 25 percent falls in the exaltation and magnification space. Most likely the first is more, and the second is less.

If we're assuming, conservatively speaking, 75 percent is transactional and 25 percent is exaltation, there needs to be a structural adjustment in the formula. If not, we will remain in a need-based prayer life, never truly living under a higher atmosphere that brings freedom and buoyancy to our lives.

Imagine then that 75 percent of your time is spent glorifying your heavenly Father, and 25 percent is asking Him for stuff. What if, and just what if, we reversed the formula and made this structural adjustment?

I know! This is not the way we were taught. I imagine you nodding, processing this. But my friend, this is the purpose of the *30 Days in His Glory Meditations and Devotional*. We have to have a new map, I say, pointing to a new operating system for the end days that we are in.

GETTING READY FOR A VACATION

So I lay before you a challenge. Take a 30-day vacation from your prayer needs! Yes, you are reading that correctly.

Years ago, a movie came out called *What About Bob?* Perhaps you saw this hilarious movie. Bob is a needy guy, acutely compulsive, and has burned out a long list of psychiatrists trying to find help. Bob found no help in the conventional world of psychiatry until one day he came across an up-and-coming notable psychiatrist. He gave Bob the most unconventional, mind-blowing solution: "Bob, take a vacation from your problems." Bob was thrilled with this new and unconventional advice. Well, you need to see the movie for what unfolds and get ready for an enjoyable time.

The point is, take a vacation from your needs.

But can you trust your heavenly Father?

Do you trust Him enough to leave your prayer needs with Him for that period?

Is God big enough, sufficient enough to sustain your losses and pressures for a period of one month?

Are you willing to surrender your hold upon your prayer needs and allow your Father to keep them during this time? Here is how we begin!

17

FINAL WORD AND INSTRUCTIONS

TO RECEIVE THE BEST START, FIRST THING EACH MORN-
ing pray the elevation psalms that are provided in the
prayer guide at the end of this book. If you have the
urge to ask God for something, *stop!* Catch yourself and
begin again.

In the beginning it will feel awkward. Press through it!
It's best to take this journey with a prayer partner, a friend,
or spouse. You can coach each other forward and hold one
another accountable. But it is not essential.

Should you find yourself merely reading the selection
of psalms, *stop* and *start* again. Make the psalmist's words
your personal prayers. Pray them back to God. Personalize

them as your own. You may even choose to highlight them in your own Bible or take the supplemental prayer book with you. You can also download them for free once you have purchased the entire offering. The download is available at Sid Roth Ministries, *It's Supernatural.*

Once you start, engage no further devotions or reading for the rest of day. Resist. Let the morning marinate. Press through. This will allow your morning devotion to saturate your soul throughout the day. I promise you, you will begin to step into the transformational realm by creating what I call "transformational space" in your prayer life.

The psalms provided in this book will help you to catch the rhythm of exaltation and magnification so that it becomes second nature. Your soul will be saturated with a new vocabulary. Born in you will be a heavenly poet emerging like a butterfly breaking free from its cocoon. Essentially, you will starve your soul of the natural order by submerging it in heavenly meditations in order to bring your soul back into alignment with Heaven!

Also, don't worry about hearing from God during this time. God will speak to you, so have a journal ready. He cannot resist speaking to His children. But remember, you are not there for any transactional need or want.

By *combining* the ancient wisdom and words of the psalmist, who better to lead us into an adventure like this than the psalmist? The Psalms is the handbook of God's glory, as well as the soul. So find a comfortable place or chair to sit in the morning for your time with God for 30 days. Allow God to guide you with the psalmist's words; each day will feel as though you are breathing the atmosphere of Heaven.

What Time Is Best?

I've found that the morning yields the greatest rewards. When all is calm and quiet, the morning is the best time to reflect on the magnification and glory of God. When our surroundings are quiet, our minds and souls are too, which is the opportune time to allow the Lord to speak. Note what the Bible reveals about the mornings.

> *Let me hear in the morning of your steadfast love, for in you I trust. Make me know the way I should go, for to you I lift up my soul* (Psalm 143:8 ESV).
>
> *I will sing of your strength; I will sing aloud of your steadfast love in the morning. For you have been to me a fortress and a refuge in the day of my distress* (Psalm 59:16 ESV).
>
> *But I, O Lord, cry to you; in the morning my prayer comes before you* (Psalm 88:13 ESV).
>
> *Satisfy us in the morning with your steadfast love, that we may rejoice and be glad all our days* (Psalm 90:14 ESV).
>
> *I rise before dawn and cry for help; I hope in your words* (Psalm 119:147 ESV).

Review Your 30 Days in His Glory

1. No praise: Praise is "I" centered. We are always thanking Him for what He has done for me and us. This is not the time for that—at least for the next 30 days.

2. No petition: Petition is "I" centered and transactional: "Lord please help me, deliver us, and alleviate my situation." Again, this is not the time for that—at least for the next 30 days.

3. Yes, only glory psalms: Glory psalms are "God" centered. There is no *I, we, my, mine.* Glory contains only "He," "You, Lord."

"Lord, You are glorious and majestic in all Your ways." "You set the stars in place and call them by name." "From day unto day and night unto night You are there." "From eternities past to the eternities that await Your creation, you shall always be upon Your glorious throne." "Nothing compares to Your greatness."

4. Begin the same time every morning: Whatever time you are accustomed to spending with God, end it for the day. Do no further reading for the remainder of the day, and allow the Holy Spirit to wash over you with the mediations of the morning.

5. After three days or so, you will begin to sense a different perception of your day. God the Creator will begin to permeate your mind. You will be more perceptive of His handprint everywhere.

6. Remember: For 30 days you will only be magnifying and enlarging God by elevation and magnification psalms. As you catch the rhythm, begin your own psalms to God. Write them in your journal. Let your meditations flow from your lips to magnify and elevate God in your life. This may take a week or so!

7. When you are set free and have entered the transformational space with God, help someone else get set free!

8. If you are willing to commit every morning for 30 days to the Lord, He will begin to absorb you, and you will begin to absorb Him. You will reboot your spiritual system, and your soul will come into daily alignment with His glorious presence. You will discover that new operating system that I speak about in the book.

Before you begin this Heavenly Soul Cleanse, pray the two preparatory prayers of the words of the Apostle Paul that follow. Important words have been highlighted, with liberty taken for certain emphasis. These prayers will be the last petitions and requests that you make before you begin the 30 Days in His Glory Meditation.

Pauls Prayers
(Amplified Bible unless noted/personalized)

> **Ephesians 1:17-20, 2:6 (Passion Translation/ Living Bible/Amplified and Amplified Classic; special emphasis added)**
>
> *"I pray that the FATHER of GLORY, the GOD of my LORD JESUS the MESSIAH, would IMPART to me the RICHES of the SPIRIT of WISDOM and the SPIRIT of REVELATION to*

KNOW HIM through my DEEPENING INTI-MACY with Him. I pray that the LIGHT of GOD will illuminate the eyes of my imagination (INNERMOST BEING), FLOODING me with LIGHT, UNTIL I experience the FULL REVELATION of the FUTURE to which He is calling me to. I pray that I will CONTINUALLY EXPERIENCE the IMMEASURABLE GREATNESS of GOD'S POWER made available to me THROUGH FAITH. Then my LIFE will be an ADVERTISEMENT of this IMMENSE POWER as it works through me!

"This is the SAME mighty power that was released when GOD raised MESSIAH from the dead and (SEATED Him) EXALTED Him to the place of HIGHEST HONOR and SUPREME AUTHORITY in the heavenly realm! And He raised me up together with Him [when I believed], and giving me the position of an adopted heir of His GLORY, and seating me with Him in the heavenly places, [because I am] in Messiah Jesus."

Ephesians 3:16-20 (Passion Translation)
"...I pray that GOD would unveil WITHIN me the UNLIMITED RICHES of His GLORY and FAVOR until HIS SUPERNATURAL STRENGTH floods my INNERMOST BEING.

"...I pray for HIS DIVINE MIGHT and EXPLOSIVE POWER....to CONSTANTLY use MY FAITH, and the LIFE of MESSIAH that will be released deep INSIDE me.

"...I pray that the resting place of HIS LOVE will become the very SOURCE and ROOT of my LIFE. THEN I will be empowered to discover what every child of God experiences—the Great Magnitude of the ASTONISHING LOVE of MESSIAH in all its dimensions. That it is deeply intimate and far-reaching Enduring and Inclusive of all of His GOODNESS. That HIS ENDLESS LOVE is BEYOND MEASUREMENT and Transcends my Understanding.

This EXTRAVAGANT LOVE pours INTO me UNTIL I am FILLED TO OVERFLOWING with the FULLNESS of GOD! I WILL NOT DOUBT GOD'S MIGHTY POWER to WORK IN me now in order to accomplish ALL that I am about to receive.

He and He alone will achieve INFINITELY MORE than my GREATEST REQUEST; my MOST UNBELIEVABLE DREAM that EXCEEDS my WILDEST IMAGINATION!

GOD, YOU will OUTDO THEM ALL, BY YOUR MIRACULOUS POWER CONSTANTLY ENERGIZES me."

30 Days in His Glory

MEDITATIONS AND DEVOTIONAL

Psalm 8:1-2

O Lord, our Lord, your majestic name fills the earth! Your glory is higher than the heavens. You have taught children and infants to tell of your strength, silencing your enemies and all who oppose you (NLT).

Psalm 8:3-9

When I look at the night sky and see the work of your fingers—the moon and the stars you set in place—what are mere mortals that you should think about them, human beings that you should care for them? Yet you made them only a little lower than God and crowned them with glory and honor. You gave them charge of everything you made, putting all things under their authority— the flocks and the herds and all the wild animals, the birds in the sky, the fish in the sea, and every-thing that swims the ocean currents. O Lord, our Lord, your majestic name fills the earth! (NLT)

Psalm 9:1-11

I will praise you, Lord, with all my heart; I will tell of all the marvelous things you have done. I will be filled with joy because of you. I will sing praises to your name, O Most High. ...You have rebuked the nations and destroyed the wicked; you have erased their names for-ever. The enemy is finished, in endless ruins; the cities you uprooted are now forgotten. But the Lord reigns forever, executing judgment from his throne. He will judge the world with justice and rule the nations with fairness. The Lord is a shelter for the oppressed, a refuge in times of trouble. Those who know your name trust in you, for you, O Lord, do not abandon those who search for you. Sing praises to the

*Lord who reigns in Jerusalem. Tell the world
about his unforgettable deeds* (NLT).

Psalm 10:16-18

*Jehovah [is] king to the age, and for ever, the
nations have perished out of His land! The
desire of the humble Thou hast heard, O Jehovah. Thou preparest their heart; Thou causest
Thine ear to attend, to judge the fatherless
and bruised: He addeth no more to oppress—
man of the earth!*

Psalm 11:3-8

*"The foundations of law and order have col-
lapsed. What can the righteous do?" But the
Lord is in his holy Temple; the Lord still rules
from heaven. He watches everyone closely,
examining every person on earth. The Lord
examines both the righteous and the wicked.
He hates those who love violence. He will
rain down blazing coals and burning sulfur
on the wicked, punishing them with scorch-
ing winds. For the righteous Lord loves
justice. The virtuous will see his face* (NLT).

Psalm 18:1-3

*I love you, Lord; you are my strength. The
Lord is my rock, my fortress, and my savior;*

my God is my rock, in whom I find protection. He is my shield, the power that saves me, and my place of safety. I called on the Lord, who is worthy of praise, and he saved me from my enemies (NLT).

Psalm 18:7-15

And shake and tremble doth the earth, and foundations of hills are troubled. And they shake—because He hath wrath. Gone up hath smoke by His nostrils, and fire from His mouth consumeth, coals have been kindled by it. And He inclineth the heavens, and cometh down, and thick darkness [is] under His feet. And He rideth on a cherub, and doth fly, and He flieth on wings of wind. He maketh darkness His secret place, round about Him His tabernacle, darkness of waters, thick clouds of the skies. From the brightness over-against Him His thick clouds have passed on, hail and coals of fire. And thunder in the heavens doth Jehovah, and the Most High giveth forth His voice, hail and coals of fire. And He sendeth His arrows and scattereth them, and much lightning, and crusheth them. And seen are the streams of waters, and revealed are foundations of the earth. From Thy rebuke, O

Jehovah, from the breath of the spirit of Thine anger (YLT).

Psalm 18:25-36

To the faithful you show yourself faithful; to those with integrity you show integrity. To the pure you show yourself pure, but to the crooked you show yourself shrewd. You rescue the humble, but you humiliate the proud. You light a lamp for me. The Lord, my God, lights up my darkness. In your strength I can crush an army; with my God I can scale any wall.

God's way is perfect. All the Lord's promises prove true. He is a shield for all who look to him for protection. For who is God except the Lord? Who but our God is a solid rock? God arms me with strength, and he makes my way perfect. He makes me as surefooted as a deer, enabling me to stand on mountain heights. He trains my hands for battle; he strengthens my arm to draw a bronze bow. You have given me your shield of victory. Your right hand supports me; your help has made me great. You have made a wide path for my feet to keep them from slipping (NLT).

Psalm 19:1-11

The heavens proclaim the glory of God. The skies display his craftsmanship. Day after day they continue to speak; night after night they make him known. They speak without a sound or word; their voice is never heard. Yet their message has gone throughout the earth, and their words to all the world.

God has made a home in the heavens for the sun. It bursts forth like a radiant bridegroom after his wedding. It rejoices like a great athlete eager to run the race. The sun rises at one end of the heavens and follows its course to the other end. Nothing can hide from its heat.

The instructions of the Lord are perfect, reviving the soul. The decrees of the Lord are trustworthy, making wise the simple. The commandments of the Lord are right, bringing joy to the heart. The commands of the Lord are clear, giving insight for living. Reverence for the Lord is pure, lasting forever. The laws of the Lord are true; each one is fair. They are more desirable than gold, even the finest gold. They are sweeter than honey, even honey dripping from the comb. They are a warning to your servant, a great reward for those who obey them (NLT).

Psalm 24:1-10

The earth is the Lord's, and everything in it. The world and all its people belong to him. For he laid the earth's foundation on the seas and built it on the ocean depths.

Who may climb the mountain of the Lord? Who may stand in his holy place? Only those whose hands and hearts are pure, who do not worship idols and never tell lies. They will receive the Lord's blessing and have a right relationship with God their savior. Such people may seek you and worship in your presence, O God of Jacob.

Open up, ancient gates! Open up, ancient doors, and let the King of glory enter. Who is the King of glory? The Lord, strong and mighty; the Lord, invincible in battle. Open up, ancient gates! Open up, ancient doors, and let the King of glory enter. Who is the King of glory, The Lord of Heaven's Armies— he is the King of glory (NLT).

Psalm 25:8-10

The Lord is good and does what is right; he shows the proper path to those who go astray.

He leads the humble in doing right, teaching
them his way. The Lord leads with unfailing
love and faithfulness all who keep his covenant and obey his demands (NLT).

Psalm 29:1-11

Honor the Lord, you heavenly beings; honor
the Lord for his glory and strength. Honor the
Lord for the glory of his name. Worship the
Lord in the splendor of his holiness. The voice
of the Lord echoes above the sea. The God of
glory thunders. The Lord thunders over the
mighty sea. The voice of the Lord is powerful; the voice of the Lord is majestic. The voice
of the Lord splits the mighty cedars; the Lord
shatters the cedars of Lebanon. He makes
Lebanon's mountains skip like a calf; he
makes Mount Hermon leap like a young wild
ox. The voice of the Lord strikes with bolts
of lightning. The voice of the Lord makes the
barren wilderness quake; the Lord shakes the
wilderness of Kadesh. The voice of the Lord
twists mighty oaks and strips the forests bare.
In his Temple everyone shouts, "Glory!" The
Lord rules over the floodwaters. The Lord
reigns as king forever. The Lord gives his
people strength. The Lord blesses them with
peace (NLT).

Psalm 31:19-20

How great is the goodness you have stored up for those who fear you. You lavish it on those who come to you for protection, blessing them before the watching world. You hide them in the shelter of your presence, safe from those who conspire against them. You shelter them in your presence, far from accusing tongues (NLT).

Psalm 33:6-22

The Lord merely spoke, and the heavens were created. He breathed the word, and all the stars were born. He assigned the sea its boundaries and locked the oceans in vast reservoirs. Let the whole world fear the Lord, and let everyone stand in awe of him. For when he spoke, the world began! It appeared at his command.

The Lord frustrates the plans of the nations and thwarts all their schemes. But the Lord's plans stand firm forever; his intentions can never be shaken.

What joy for the nation whose God is the Lord, whose people he has chosen as his inheritance.

The Lord looks down from heaven and sees the whole human race. From his throne he observes all who live on the earth. He made their hearts, so he understands everything they do. The best-equipped army cannot save a king, nor is great strength enough to save a warrior. Don't count on your warhorse to give you victory—for all its strength, it cannot save you.

But the Lord watches over those who fear him, those who rely on his unfailing love. He rescues them from death and keeps them alive in times of famine.

We put our hope in the Lord. He is our help and our shield. In him our hearts rejoice, for we trust in his holy name. Let your unfailing love surround us, Lord, for our hope is in you alone (NLT).

Psalm 36:5-10

Your unfailing love, O Lord, is as vast as the heavens; your faithfulness reaches beyond the clouds. Your righteousness is like the mighty mountains, your justice like the ocean depths. You care for people and animals alike, O Lord. How precious is your unfailing love, O God! All humanity finds shelter in the shadow of your wings. You feed them from

*the abundance of your own house, letting
them drink from your river of delights. For
you are the fountain of life, the light by which
we see. Pour out your unfailing love on those
who love you; give justice to those with honest
hearts* (NLT).

Psalm 39:5-7

*"You have made my life no longer than the
width of my hand. My entire lifetime is just
a moment to you; at best, each of us is but a
breath." We are merely moving shadows, and
all our busy rushing ends in nothing. We heap
up wealth, not knowing who will spend it.
And so, Lord, where do I put my hope? My
only hope is in you* (NLT).

Psalm 40:4-9

*Oh, the joys of those who trust the Lord, who
have no confidence in the proud or in those
who worship idols. O Lord my God, you have
performed many wonders for us. Your plans
for us are too numerous to list. You have no
equal. If I tried to recite all your wonderful
deeds, I would never come to the end of them.
You take no delight in sacrifices or offerings. Now that you have made me listen, I
finally understand—you don't require burnt*

offerings or sin offerings. Then I said, "Look, I have come. As is written about me in the Scriptures: I take joy in doing your will, my God, for your instructions are written on my heart.

I have told all your people about your justice. I have not been afraid to speak out, as you, O Lord, well know (NLT).

Psalm 40:16

But may all who search for you be filled with joy and gladness in you. May those who love your salvation repeatedly shout, "The Lord is great!" (NLT)

Psalm 45:1

My heart is stirred by a noble theme as I recite my verses for the king; my tongue is the pen of a skillful writer.

Psalm 45:1-9

Beautiful words stir my heart. I will recite a lovely poem about the king, for my tongue is like the pen of a skillful poet.

You are the most handsome of all. Gracious words stream from your lips. God himself has blessed you forever. Put on your sword, O mighty warrior! You are so glorious, so majestic! In your majesty, ride out to victory, defending truth, humility, and justice. Go forth to perform awe-inspiring deeds! Your arrows are sharp, piercing your enemies' hearts. The nations fall beneath your feet.

Your throne, O God, endures forever and ever. You rule with a scepter of justice. You love justice and hate evil. Therefore God, your God, has anointed you, pouring out the oil of joy on you more than on anyone else. Myrrh, aloes, and cassia perfume your robes. In ivory palaces the music of strings entertains you. Kings' daughters are among your noble women. At your right side stands the queen, wearing jewelry of finest gold from Ophir! (NLT)

Psalm 46:1-11

God is our refuge and strength, always ready to help in times of trouble. So we will not fear when earthquakes come and the mountains crumble into the sea. Let the oceans roar and foam. Let the mountains tremble as the waters surge!

A river brings joy to the city of our God, the sacred home of the Most High. God dwells in that city; it cannot be destroyed. From the very break of day, God will protect it. The nations are in chaos, and their kingdoms crumble! God's voice thunders, and the earth melts! The Lord of Heaven's Armies is here among us; the God of Israel is our fortress.

Come, see the glorious works of the Lord: See how he brings destruction upon the world. He causes wars to end throughout the earth. He breaks the bow and snaps the spear; he burns the shields with fire.

"Be still, and know that I am God! I will be honored by every nation. I will be honored throughout the world."

The Lord of Heaven's Armies is here among us; the God of Israel is our fortress (NLT).

Psalm 48:1-3

How great is the Lord, how deserving of praise, in the city of our God, which sits on his holy mountain! It is high and magnificent; the whole earth rejoices to see it! Mount Zion, the holy mountain, is the city of the great King! God himself is in Jerusalem's towers, revealing himself as its defender (NLT).

Psalm 48:8-11

We had heard of the city's glory, but now we have seen it ourselves—the city of the Lord of Heaven's Armies. It is the city of our God; he will make it safe forever. O God, we meditate on your unfailing love as we worship in your Temple. As your name deserves, O God, you will be praised to the ends of the earth. Your strong right hand is filled with victory. Let the people on Mount Zion rejoice. Let all the towns of Judah be glad because of your justice (NLT).

Psalm 50:1-6

The Lord, the Mighty One, is God, and he has spoken; he has summoned all humanity from where the sun rises to where it sets. From Mount Zion, the perfection of beauty, God shines in glorious radiance. Our God approaches, and he is not silent. Fire devours everything in his way, and a great storm rages around him. He calls on the heavens above and earth below to witness the judgment of his people. "Bring my faithful people to me—those who made a covenant with me by giving sacrifices." Then let the heavens proclaim his justice, for God himself will be the judge (NLT).

Psalm 65:1-13

What mighty praise, O God, belongs to you in Zion. We will fulfill our vows to you, for you answer our prayers. All of us must come to you. Though we are overwhelmed by our sins, you forgive them all. What joy for those you choose to bring near, those who live in your holy courts. What festivities await us inside your holy Temple.

You faithfully answer our prayers with awesome deeds, O God our savior. You are the hope of everyone on earth, even those who sail on distant seas. You formed the mountains by your power and armed yourself with mighty strength. You quieted the raging oceans with their pounding waves and silenced the shouting of the nations. Those who live at the ends of the earth stand in awe of your wonders. From where the sun rises to where it sets, you inspire shouts of joy.

You take care of the earth and water it, making it rich and fertile. The river of God has plenty of water; it provides a bountiful harvest of grain, for you have ordered it so. You drench the plowed ground with rain, melting the clods and leveling the ridges. You soften the earth with showers and bless its abundant crops. You crown the year with a bountiful harvest; even the hard pathways overflow with abundance. The grasslands of the wilderness become a lush pasture, and the hillsides blossom with joy. The meadows are

*clothed with flocks of sheep, and the valleys
are carpeted with grain. They all shout and
sing for joy!* (NLT)

Psalm 66:1-7

*Shout joyful praises to God, all the earth! Sing
about the glory of his name! Tell the world how
glorious he is. Say to God, "How awesome are
your deeds! Your enemies cringe before your
mighty power. Everything on earth will worship you; they will sing your praises, shouting
your name in glorious songs." Come and see
what our God has done, what awesome miracles he performs for people! He made a dry
path through the Red Sea, and his people
went across on foot. There we rejoiced in him.
For by his great power he rules forever. He
watches every movement of the nations; let no
rebel rise in defiance* (NLT).

Psalm 67:1-7

*May God be merciful and bless us. May his
face smile with favor on us. May your ways
be known throughout the earth, your saving
power among people everywhere. May the
nations praise you, O God. Yes, may all the
nations praise you. Let the whole world sing
for joy, because you govern the nations with*

justice and guide the people of the whole world. May the nations praise you, O God. Yes, may all the nations praise you. Then the earth will yield its harvests, and God, our God, will richly bless us. Yes, God will bless us, and people all over the world will fear him (NLT).

Psalm 68:1-14,17-20

Rise up, O God, and scatter your enemies. Let those who hate God run for their lives. Blow them away like smoke. Melt them like wax in a fire. Let the wicked perish in the presence of God. But let the godly rejoice. Let them be glad in God's presence. Let them be filled with joy. Sing praises to God and to his name! Sing loud praises to him who rides the clouds. His name is the Lord—rejoice in his presence!

Father to the fatherless, defender of widows— this is God, whose dwelling is holy. God places the lonely in families; he sets the prisoners free and gives them joy. But he makes the rebellious live in a sun-scorched land.

O God, when you led your people out from Egypt, when you marched through the dry wasteland, the earth trembled, and the heavens poured down rain before you, the God of Sinai, before God, the God of Israel. You sent abundant rain, O God, to refresh the weary land. There your people finally settled, and with a bountiful harvest, O God, you provided for your needy people.

...The mountains of Bashan are majestic, with many peaks stretching high into the sky. Why do you look with envy, O rugged mountains, at Mount Zion, where God has chosen to live, where the Lord himself will live forever?

Surrounded by unnumbered thousands of chariots, the Lord came from Mount Sinai into his sanctuary. When you ascended to the heights, you led a crowd of captives. You received gifts from the people, even from those who rebelled against you. Now the Lord God will live among us there.

Praise the Lord; praise God our savior! For each day he carries us in his arms. Our God is a God who saves! The Sovereign Lord rescues us from death (NLT).

Psalm 69:34-36

Let heaven and earth praise him, the seas and all that move in them, for God will save Zion and rebuild the cities of Judah. Then people will settle there and possess it; the children of his servants will inherit it, and those who love his name will dwell there.

Psalm 77:13-20

O God, your ways are holy. Is there any god as mighty as you? You are the God of great wonders! You demonstrate your awesome power among the nations. By your strong arm, you redeemed your people, the descendants of Jacob and Joseph. When the Red Sea saw you, O God, its waters looked and trembled! The sea quaked to its very depths. The clouds poured down rain; the thunder rumbled in the sky. Your arrows of lightning flashed. Your thunder roared from the whirlwind; the lightning lit up the world! The earth trembled and shook. Your road led through the sea, your pathway through the mighty waters—a pathway no one knew was there! You led your people along that road like a flock of sheep, with Moses and Aaron as their shepherds (NLT).

Psalm 84:1-5

How lovely is your dwelling place, O Lord of Heaven's Armies. I long, yes, I faint with longing to enter the courts of the Lord. With my whole being, body and soul, I will shout joyfully to the living God. Even the sparrow finds a home, and the swallow builds her nest and raises her young at a place near your altar,

O Lord of Heaven's Armies, my King and my God! What joy for those who can live in your house, always singing your praises. What joy for those whose strength comes from the Lord, who have set their minds on a pilgrimage to Jerusalem (NLT).

Psalm 84:10-12

A single day in your courts is better than a thousand anywhere else! I would rather be a gatekeeper in the house of my God than live the good life in the homes of the wicked. For the Lord God is our sun and our shield. He gives us grace and glory. The Lord will withhold no good thing from those who do what is right. O Lord of Heaven's Armies, what joy for those who trust in you (NLT).

Psalm 85:10-13

Unfailing love and truth have met together. Righteousness and peace have kissed! Truth springs up from the earth, and righteousness smiles down from heaven. Yes, the Lord pours down his blessings. Our land will yield its bountiful harvest. Righteousness goes as a herald before him, preparing the way for his steps (NLT).

Psalm 87:1-3

On the holy mountain stands the city founded by the Lord. He loves the city of Jerusalem more than any other city in Israel. O city of God, what glorious things are said of you! (NLT)

Psalm 89:9-18

You rule the oceans. You subdue their storm-tossed waves. You crushed the great sea monster. You scattered your enemies with your mighty arm. The heavens are yours, and the earth is yours; everything in the world is yours—you created it all. You created north and south. Mount Tabor and Mount Hermon praise your name. Powerful is your arm! Strong is your hand! Your right hand is lifted high in glorious strength. Righteousness and justice are the foundation of your throne. Unfailing love and truth walk before you as attendants. Happy are those who hear the joyful call to worship, for they will walk in the light of your presence, Lord. They rejoice all day long in your wonderful reputation. They exult in your righteousness. You are their glorious strength. It pleases you to make us strong. Yes, our protection comes from the Lord, and he, the Holy One of Israel, has given us our king (NLT).

Psalm 90:1-6

Lord, through all the generations you have been our home! Before the mountains were born, before you gave birth to the earth and the world, from beginning to end, you are God. You turn people back to dust, saying, "Return to dust, you mortals!" For you, a thousand years are as a passing day, as brief as a few night hours. You sweep people away like dreams that disappear. They are like grass that springs up in the morning. In the morning it blooms and flourishes, but by evening it is dry and withered (NLT).

Psalm 90:11-12

Who can comprehend the power of your anger? Your wrath is as awesome as the fear you deserve. Teach us to realize the brevity of life, so that we may grow in wisdom (NLT).

Psalm 93:1-5

The Lord is king! He is robed in majesty. Indeed, the Lord is robed in majesty and armed with strength. The world stands firm and cannot be shaken.

Your throne, O Lord, has stood from time immemorial. You yourself are from the everlasting past. The floods have risen up, O Lord. The floods have roared like thunder; the floods have lifted their pounding waves. But mightier than the violent raging of the seas, mightier than the breakers on the shore—the Lord above is mightier than these! Your royal laws cannot be changed. Your reign, O Lord, is holy forever and ever (NLT).

Psalm 95:1-7

Come, let us sing to the Lord! Let us shout joyfully to the Rock of our salvation. Let us come to him with thanksgiving. Let us sing psalms of praise to him. For the Lord is a great God, a great King above all gods. He holds in his hands the depths of the earth and the mightiest mountains. The sea belongs to him, for he made it. His hands formed the dry land, too.

Come, let us worship and bow down. Let us kneel before the Lord our maker, for he is our God. We are the people he watches over, the flock under his care (NLT).

Psalm 96:1-6

Sing a new song to the Lord! Let the whole earth sing to the Lord! Sing to the Lord;

praise his name. Each day proclaim the good news that he saves. Publish his glorious deeds among the nations. Tell everyone about the amazing things he does. Great is the Lord! He is most worthy of praise! He is to be feared above all gods. The gods of other nations are mere idols, but the Lord made the heavens! Honor and majesty surround him; strength and beauty fill his sanctuary (NLT).

Psalm 96:4-13

For great is the Lord and most worthy of praise; he is to be feared above all gods. For all the gods of the nations are idols, but the Lord made the heavens. Splendor and majesty are before him; strength and glory are in his sanctuary.

Ascribe to the Lord, all you families of nations, ascribe to the Lord glory and strength. Ascribe to the Lord the glory due his name; bring an offering and come into his courts. Worship the Lord in the splendor of his holiness; tremble before him, all the earth. Say among the nations, "The Lord reigns." The world is firmly established, it cannot be moved; he will judge the peoples with equity.

Let the heavens rejoice, let the earth be glad; let the sea resound, and all that is in it. Let

the fields be jubilant, and everything in them;
let all the trees of the forest sing for joy. Let all
creation rejoice before the Lord, for he comes,
he comes to judge the earth. He will judge the
world in righteousness and the peoples in his
faithfulness.

Psalm 97:1-12

The Lord is king! Let the earth rejoice! Let the
farthest coastlands be glad. Dark clouds surround him. Righteousness and justice are the
foundation of his throne. Fire spreads ahead
of him and burns up all his foes. His lightning flashes out across the world. The earth
sees and trembles. The mountains melt like
wax before the Lord, before the Lord of all the
earth. The heavens proclaim his righteousness; every nation sees his glory. Those who
worship idols are disgraced—all who brag
about their worthless gods—for every god
must bow to him. Jerusalem has heard and
rejoiced, and all the towns of Judah are glad
because of your justice, O Lord! For you, O
Lord, are supreme over all the earth; you are
exalted far above all gods.

You who love the Lord, hate evil! He protects
the lives of his godly people and rescues them
from the power of the wicked. Light shines

on the godly, and joy on those whose hearts are right. May all who are godly rejoice in the Lord and praise His holy name! (NLT)

Psalm 99:1-5

The Lord is king! Let the nations tremble! He sits on his throne between the cherubim. Let the whole earth quake! The Lord sits in majesty in Jerusalem, exalted above all the nations. Let them praise your great and awesome name. Your name is holy! Mighty King, lover of justice, you have established fairness. You have acted with justice and righteousness throughout Israel. Exalt the Lord our God! Bow low before his feet, for he is holy! (NLT)

Psalm 103:1-22

Bless, O my soul, Jehovah, and all my inward parts—His Holy Name. Bless, O my soul, Jehovah, and forget not all His benefits, who is forgiving all thine iniquities, who is healing all thy diseases, who is redeeming from destruction thy life, who is crowning thee— kindness and mercies, who is satisfying with good thy desire, renew itself as an eagle doth thy youth.

Jehovah is doing righteousness and judgments for all the oppressed. He maketh known His

*ways to Moses, to the sons of Israel His acts.
Merciful and gracious [is] Jehovah, slow to
anger, and abundant in mercy. Not for ever
doth He strive, nor to the age doth He watch.
Not according to our sins hath He done to us,
nor according to our iniquities hath He con-
ferred benefits upon us.*

*For, as the height of the heavens [is] above the
earth, His kindness hath been mighty over
those fearing Him. As the distance of east
from west He hath put far from us our trans-
gressions. As a father hath mercy on sons,
Jehovah hath mercy on those fearing Him.
For He hath known our frame, remembering
that we [are] dust. Mortal man! as grass [are]
his days, as a flower of the field so he flour-
isheth; for a wind hath passed over it, and it
is not. And its place doth not discern it any
more. And the kindness of Jehovah [is] from
age even unto age on those fearing Him, and
His righteousness to sons' sons, to those keeping His covenant, and to those remembering
His precepts to do them.*

*Jehovah in the heavens hath established His
throne, and His kingdom over all hath ruled.
Bless Jehovah, ye His messengers, mighty in
power—doing His word, to hearken to the
voice of His Word. Bless Jehovah, all ye His*

hosts, His ministers—doing His pleasure. Bless Jehovah, all ye His works. In all places of His dominion. Bless, O my soul, Jehovah! (YLT)

Psalm 104:1-34

Let all that I am praise the Lord. O Lord my God, how great you are! You are robed with honor and majesty. You are dressed in a robe of light. You stretch out the starry curtain of the heavens; you lay out the rafters of your home in the rain clouds. You make the clouds your chariot; you ride upon the wings of the wind. The winds are your messengers; flames of fire are your servants.

You placed the world on its foundation so it would never be moved. You clothed the earth with floods of water, water that covered even the mountains. At your command, the water fled; at the sound of your thunder, it hurried away. Mountains rose and valleys sank to the levels you decreed. Then you set a firm boundary for the seas, so they would never again cover the earth.

You make springs pour water into the ravines, so streams gush down from the mountains. They provide water for all the animals, and the wild donkeys quench their thirst. The birds nest beside the streams and sing among the branches of the trees. You send rain on the mountains from your heavenly home, and you fill the earth with the fruit of your labor. You cause grass to grow for the livestock and plants for people to use. You allow them to produce food from the earth—wine to make them glad, olive oil to soothe their skin, and bread to give them strength. The trees of the Lord are well cared for—the cedars of Lebanon that he planted. There the birds make their nests, and the storks make their homes in the cypresses. High in the mountains live the wild goats, and the rocks form a refuge for the hyraxes.

You made the moon to mark the seasons, and the sun knows when to set. You send the darkness, and it becomes night, when all the forest animals prowl about. Then the young lions roar for their prey, stalking the food provided by God. At dawn they slink back into their dens to rest. Then people go off to their work, where they labor until evening.

O Lord, what a variety of things you have made! In wisdom you have made them all. The earth is full of your creatures. Here is the ocean, vast and wide, teeming with life of every kind, both large and small. See the ships sailing along, and Leviathan, which you made to play in the sea.

They all depend on you to give them food as they need it. When you supply it, they gather it. You open your hand to feed them, and they are richly satisfied. But if you turn away from them, they panic. When you take away their breath, they die and turn again to dust. When you give them your breath, life is created, and you renew the face of the earth.

May the glory of the Lord continue forever! The Lord takes pleasure in all he has made! The earth trembles at his glance; the mountains smoke at his touch.

I will sing to the Lord as long as I live. I will praise my God to my last breath! May all my thoughts be pleasing to him, for I rejoice in the Lord (NLT).

Psalm 107:8-9

Let them praise the Lord for his great love and for the wonderful things he has done for them. For he satisfies the thirsty and fills the hungry with good things (NLT).

Psalm 111:1-10

I will thank the Lord with all my heart as I meet with his godly people. How amazing are the deeds of the Lord! All who delight in him should ponder them. Everything he does reveals his glory and majesty. His righteousness never fails. He causes us to remember his wonderful works. How gracious and merciful is our Lord! He gives food to those who fear him; he always remembers his covenant. He has shown his great power to His people by giving them the lands of other nations. All he does is just and good, and all his commandments are trustworthy. They are forever true, to be obeyed faithfully and with integrity. He has paid a full ransom for his people. He has guaranteed his covenant with them forever. What a holy, awe-inspiring name he has! Fear of the Lord is the foundation of true wisdom. All who obey his commandments will grow in wisdom (NLT).

Psalm 113:1-9

Praise the Lord! Yes, give praise, O servants of the Lord. Praise the name of the Lord! Blessed be the name of the Lord now and forever. Everywhere—from east to west—praise the name of the Lord. For the Lord is high above the nations; his glory is higher than the heavens. Who can be compared with the Lord our God, who is enthroned on high? He stoops to look down on heaven and on earth. He lifts the poor from the dust and the needy from the garbage dump. He sets them among princes, even the princes of his own people! He gives the childless woman a family, making her a happy mother (NLT).

Psalm 115:16-18

The heavens belong to the Lord, but he has given the earth to all humanity. The dead cannot sing praises to the Lord, for they have gone into the silence of the grave. But we can praise the Lord both now and forever! (NLT)

Psalm 118:2-9

Let Israel say, "His steadfast love endures forever." Let the house of Aaron say, "His steadfast love endures forever." Let those who fear the Lord say, "His steadfast love endures forever." Out of my distress I called on the Lord; the Lord answered me and set me free. The Lord is on my side; I will not fear. What can man do to me? The Lord is on my side as my helper; I shall look in triumph on those who hate me. It is better to take refuge in the Lord than to trust in man. It is better to take refuge in the Lord (ESV).

Psalm 118:22-23

> The stone that the builders rejected has now become the cornerstone. This is the Lord's doing, and it is wonderful to see (NLT).

Psalms 121:1-5

> I look up to the mountains—does my help come from there? My help comes from the Lord, who made heaven and earth! He will not let you stumble; the one who watches over you will not slumber. Indeed, he who watches over Israel never slumbers or sleeps. The Lord himself watches over you! The Lord stands beside you as your protective shade (NLT).

Psalm 121:7-8

> The Lord will keep you from all harm—he will watch over your life; the Lord will watch over your coming and going both now and forevermore.

Psalm 123:1-2

> I lift my eyes to you, O God, enthroned in heaven. We keep looking to the Lord our God for his mercy, just as servants keep their eyes on their master, as a slave girl watches her mistress for the slightest signal (NLT).

Psalm 126:1-3

When the Lord brought back his exiles to Jerusalem, it was like a dream! We were filled with laughter, and we sang for joy. And the other nations said, "What amazing things the Lord has done for them." Yes, the Lord has done amazing things for us! What joy! (NLT)

Psalm 135: 5-14

I know that the Lord is great, that our Lord is greater than all gods. The Lord does whatever pleases him, in the heavens and on the earth, in the seas and all their depths. He makes clouds rise from the ends of the earth; he sends lightning with the rain and brings out the wind from his storehouses.

He struck down the firstborn of Egypt, the firstborn of people and animals. He sent his signs and wonders into your midst, Egypt, against Pharaoh and all his servants. He struck down many nations and killed mighty kings—Siphon king of the Amorites, Og king of Bashan, and all the kings of Canaan—and he gave their land as an inheritance, an inheritance to his people Israel.

Your name, Lord, endures forever, your renown, Lord, through all generations. For the Lord will vindicate his people and have compassion on his servants.

Psalm 145:3-21

Great is the Lord and most worthy of praise; his greatness no one can fathom. One generation commends your works to another; they tell of your mighty acts. They speak of the glorious splendor of your majesty—and I will meditate on your wonderful works. They tell of the power of your awesome works—and I will proclaim your great deeds. They celebrate your abundant goodness and joyfully sing of your righteousness.

The Lord is gracious and compassionate, slow to anger and rich in love. The Lord is good to all; he has compassion on all he has made. All your works praise you, Lord; your faithful people extol you. They tell of the glory of your kingdom and speak of your might, so that all people may know of your mighty acts and the glorious splendor of your kingdom.

Your kingdom is an everlasting kingdom, and your dominion endures through all generations. The Lord is trustworthy in all he promises and faithful in all he does. The Lord upholds all who fall and lifts up all who are bowed down. The eyes of all look to you, and you give them their food at the proper time. You open your hand and satisfy the desires of every living thing.

The Lord is righteous in all his ways and faithful in all he does. The Lord is near to all who call on him, to all who call on him in truth. He fulfills the desires of those who fear him; he hears their cry and saves them. The Lord watches over all who love him, but all the wicked he will destroy. My mouth will speak in praise of the Lord. Let every creature praise his holy name for ever and ever.

Psalm 146:1-10

Praise the Lord. Praise the Lord, my soul. I will praise the Lord all my life; I will sing praise to my God as long as I live. Do not put your trust in princes, in human beings, who cannot save. When their spirit departs, they return to the ground; on that very day their plans come to nothing.

Blessed are those whose help is the God of Jacob, whose hope is in the Lord their God. He is the Maker of heaven and earth, the sea, and everything in them—he remains faithful forever. He upholds the cause of the oppressed and gives food to the hungry.

The Lord sets prisoners free, the Lord gives sight to the blind, the Lord lifts up those who are bowed down, the Lord loves the righteous. The Lord watches over the foreigner and sustains the fatherless and the widow, but he frustrates the ways of the wicked. The Lord reigns forever, your God, O Zion, for all generations. Praise the Lord.

Psalm 147:1-20

Praise ye Jah! For [it is] good to praise our God, for pleasant—comely [is] praise. Building Jerusalem [is] Jehovah, the driven away of Israel He gathereth. Who is giving healing to the broken of heart, and is binding up their griefs. Appointing the number of the stars, to all them He giveth names. Great [is] our Lord, and abundant in power, of His understanding there is no narration. Jehovah is causing the meek to stand, making low the wicked unto the earth.

Answer ye to Jehovah with thanksgiving, sing ye to our God with a harp. Who is covering the heavens with clouds, who is preparing for the earth rain, who is causing grass to spring up [on] mountains, giving to the beast its food, to the young of the ravens that call. Not in the might of the horse doth He delight, not in the legs of a man is He pleased.

Jehovah is pleased with those fearing Him, with those waiting for His kindness. Glorify, O Jerusalem, Jehovah, praise thy God, O Zion. For He did strengthen the bars of thy gates, He hath blessed thy sons in thy midst. Who is making thy border peace, [with] the fat of wheat He satisfieth Thee. Who is sending forth His saying [on] earth, very speedily doth His word run.

Who is giving snow like wool, hoar-frost as ashes He scattereth. Casting forth His ice like morsels. Before His cold who doth stand? He sendeth forth His word and melteth them, He causeth His wind to blow—the waters flow. Declaring His words to Jacob, His statutes and His judgments to Israel. He hath not done so to any nation, as to judgments, they have not known them. Praise ye Jah! (YLT)

ABOUT FELIX HALPERN

Felix Halpern was born in 1952 in the Netherlands. As a child his family immigrated to the United States, where he was raised in the northern New Jersey area. Prior to full-time ministry, he established a lucrative career in the precious metals and diamond industries located in the International Diamond Center of New York City. Immersed for nearly two decades in the Orthodox and Hassidic Jewish communities, he understands well the heart of the Jewish people.

Coming from a rich Jewish heritage himself, he is also rooted in Nazi resistance. Rabbi Halpern's paternal grandfather was an Orthodox rabbi and leader of his own synagogue in Germany, and his maternal grandparents established one of the many underground resistance movements against Hitler throughout the Netherlands. It is also where his father received the knowledge and understanding of his Messiah while being hidden with other Jews, after miraculously escaping Germany.

MINISTRY TODAY

Today, Felix Halpern ministers nationally and internationally with a message of restoration between Jew and Gentile and a strong burden to bring the Father's love to the nations.

Felix Halpern serves as a nationally appointed missionary to the Jewish people, and for twenty years he and his wife Bonnie served as senior leaders of a Messianic congregation that they founded, Beth Chofesh (House of Freedom).

He pioneered the first National Jewish Fellowship of the Assemblies of God and has served the first four years as its president. He has also served as a general presbyter for the Assemblies of God, on the AG Board of Ethnicity, and also on the board of Lost Lamb Evangelistic Association.

In 2013 God provided the means to form the first Resource Office for Jewish Ministry within the Assemblies of God in the greater New York and New Jersey metropolitan region, called Metro Jewish Resources.

In 2019, out of his life and death experience and his journey into the third heaven, Chofesh Ministries (Freedom Ministries) was formed in 2020.

Felix Halpern

PO Box 3777

Wayne, NJ 07470

Email: hisglobalglory@gmail.com

Web.: www.chofesh.org

Phone: 973-461-9786